Synergogy

*A New Strategy
for Education, Training,
and Development*

Jane Srygley Mouton
Robert R. Blake

Synergogy

A New Strategy
for Education, Training,
and Development

Jossey-Bass Publishers
San Francisco • Washington • London • 1984

SYNERGOGY
A New Strategy for Education, Training, and Development
by Jane Srygley Mouton and Robert R. Blake

Library of Congress Cataloging in Publication Data

Mouton, Jane Srygley.
    Synergogy : a new strategy for education, training,
and development.

    Bibliography: p. 184
    Includes index.
    1. Learning, Psychology of. 2. Motivation in
education. 3. Transfer of training. 4. Association of
ideas. I. Blake, Robert Rogers, 1918–   . II. Title.
LB1051.M7365   1984   370.15′23   83-23898
ISBN 0-87589-590-5

Manufactured in the United States of America

The paper in this book meets the guidelines for
permanence and durability of the Committee on
Production Guidelines for Book Longevity of the
Council on Library Resources.

JACKET DESIGN BY WILLI BAUM

FIRST EDITION

Code 8404

A joint publication in
The Jossey-Bass Management Series
and
The Jossey-Bass Higher Education Series

Contents

Preface

≈◦◦◦◦◦◦◦◦◦≈

The base of useful knowledge is constantly growing at an ever-accelerating rate. The task of education, training, and development in the 1980s is to help people acquire and use this information as effectively as possible.

The current debate among educators reflects a widespread concern for how learning is best facilitated. Much of this debate concentrates on improving the traditional methods of delivering education: increasing teachers' salaries, shifting to a merit basis of compensation, extending classroom contact hours, and so on. But our experience and analyses suggest that the weaknesses of education are inherent in the delivery systems now in use—and that proposed adjustments in those systems do not alleviate those weaknesses. Instead, in this book we present *synergogy,* a relatively new approach that constitutes a constructive alternative to the national endeavor to improve education.

Synergogy is derived from two Greek words: *synergos* ("working together") and *agogus* ("leader of"), which has come to mean "teacher." *Synergogy* thus refers to "working together for shared teaching."* Synergogy is a systematic approach to learning in which the members of small teams learn from one another through structured interactions; thus the idea of synergy in learning. Challenge and stimulation are created through social situations under which real as well as felt needs for learning can be satisfied. The instructor or learning administrator provides educational materials from which knowledge or insights can be acquired and creates designs—instructions for team action—that stimulate learning.

Synergogy is an alternative mode of education that should be examined in the light of the benefits and limitations of two traditional approaches, pedagogy and andragogy. Pedagogy is the most standard classroom model: an instructor who is an expert in the subject under study lectures, gives assignments, tests students' achievement, and so forth. In brief, the teacher teaches and the learners passively absorb whatever they can. A key advantage of pedagogy is that it permits codified knowledge to be presented in an orderly manner. Its chief disadvantage, however, is that students are often passive and unmotivated. Andragogy (meaning "adults teaching other adults") posits a different role for the instructor. The teacher serves as a facilitator or catalyst for the learners' activities. An advantage of andragogy is that learners' motivation is enhanced through greater responsibility for and involvement in learning. But andragogic methods are often situation-dependent and cannot be applied to codify or standardize information for mass use. Synergogy builds on the best features of pedagogy and andragogy while avoiding the limitations associated with each. It does so by enabling learners to acquire codified knowledge under conditions that arouse their involvement and commitment.

This book is the first comprehensive orientation to synergogy, a presentation of its assumptions, methodologies, and applications, as well as the responses of those who have used it. We began this work thirty years ago when, as professors of so-

---

Synergagogy is technically correct, according to conventions of creating words from Greek roots, but needlessly difficult. *Synergogy* is an acceptable alternative.

cial psychology at the University of Texas, we were struck by postwar students' reactions to coursework: they found the classroom situation unstimulating, but their interests were aroused when they participated in laboratory applications of learning. Further, their laboratory efforts to apply classroom learning to lifelike problems demonstrated to them and to us how little they could use of what they had studied in the classroom. Our observations led us to investigate how to bring codified knowledge and laboratory learning methods together in a manner that motivated students to use what they had learned for solving real-life problems or for enriching their own experience.

Experiments in learning followed, and our first articles to attract much interest appeared in the early 1960s (Mouton and Blake, 1961; Blake and Mouton, 1962). These were followed by applications of the experiments to the teaching of psychology, sociology, English literature, history, fine arts, physical science, and engineering. As we began to perfect synergogic methods for university courses, our attention turned to synergogy's pertinence within industry and government. Numerous applications included problem solving and training in areas as diverse as understanding a union contract, solving crises in the cockpit of a modern jetliner, risk assessment regarding malpractice in medicine and law, and learning skills for reading a gas meter or a financial statement.

Subsequent consultations enabled us to devise applications of synergogy for use outside the United States. These experiences permitted us to explore whether the learning motivations involved were unique to industrial nations such as the United States or whether they had applications in developing countries. Synergogy has now been tested for usefulness throughout Europe and the eastern bloc nations, in Japan, in the developing countries of Southeast Asia—including the Philippines, Malaysia, Indonesia, Pakistan, and India—and throughout the Middle East, Africa, and South America.

The development and field testing of synergogy are now complete, and organized programs have been underway in universities and industrial organizations for ten years. At the culmination of this long-term effort we conclude that the synergogic designs apply across the areas of codified knowledge, are culture free, and arouse motivations that are essentially universal in character.

Synergogy has proved itself to be a comprehensive approach that can be used in the acquisition of knowledge, the examination and change of attitudes, and the acquisition of skills. Academic applications have ranged from psychology to physics, and from secondary through graduate school. Industrial and government trainers have used these methods to aid managers, supervisors, secretaries, and others to acquire both the general knowledge they need to perform effectively—such subjects as manufacturing, marketing, finance, office management, and so on—and job-specific information on topics as diverse as safety procedures in a chemical factory, principles and practices for budgetary procedures in a public agency, cost cutting in a bank, and error reduction in coding and transcribing for a data-processing system. Human resource personnel will find the methods pertinent for aiding organization members to study and change the culture and practices currently in use in their organizations.

In Chapter One, we examine education as an activity that takes place within the context of human relationships. We discuss how the authority-obedience model implicit in pedagogic relationships may impede rather than advance students' learning. Colleague-centered learning avoids this problem but replaces it with another: how to get learners to study codified knowledge without teacher direction and control. Our solution is offered in Chapter Two, which presents an overview of synergogic principles and designs. The concept of learning designs—structures within which learners teach one another—is introduced and the four basic designs are outlined. Chapters Three through Six then provide a step-by-step presentation of how to implement the four designs. The designs are described in sufficient detail so that the reader can apply them to various academic, training, or development courses. Case examples for each design illustrate various applications.

Chapter Seven focuses on the role of the learning administrator, who need not necessarily be a credentialed teacher or an academic instructor. Rather, the learning administrator executes the designs and works with learners in ways that promote their responsibility for active learning. Chapter Eight offers examples of the application of the four designs in various industrial and commercial settings in which the subject is safety education. Chapter Nine addresses academic applications.

The final chapter summarizes interviews with professional users concerning their years of experience in applying the designs in business and academic settings. The chapter concludes with an examination of synergogy's implications for the future of education, training, and development. References and a selected annotated bibliography that provides suggestions for further study complete the book.

Many individuals have contributed to our research and experiments, but five whose works are used in this presentation deserve special acknowledgment. David Clifford has exercised much initiative in demonstrating how these designs can be employed in teaching industrial personnel a wide variety of applied subjects. Duncan Murray has experimented with applications in the education and training of medical students and medical practitioners. J. E. Carroll has initiated a series of experiments that have resulted in synergogic designs to promote airline safety in the cockpit of the modern jetliner. Utho Creusen has also provided important examples of applications as they relate to selection and interviewing. Charles Hoke has been responsible for innovative applications in the university setting with graduate students. We and others have promoted similar efforts in the college setting, and elementary and secondary education projects have been conducted by many.

We also acknowledge the invaluable contribution of Larry N. Davis, who acted as editorial consultant for Jossey-Bass Publishers on the project. Our appreciation extends to all who have been engaged with us in exploring the potential of synergogy as a basis for a significant extension of education.

Austin, Texas   Jane Srygley Mouton
January 1984   Robert R. Blake

The Authors

Jane Srygley Mouton is president and cofounder of Scientific Methods, Inc., a behavioral science firm specializing in education and organization development, and was codeveloper of the concepts of the Managerial Grid, a widely known theory of leadership. Mouton received a bachelor's degree in mathematics at the University of Texas at Austin (1950), a master's degree in psychology from Florida State University (1951), and a doctoral degree in psychology from the University of Texas at Austin (1957), where she also was a faculty member. She is an associate of the American Psychological Association; a diplomate in Industrial and Organizational Psychology, American Board of Professional Psychology; and a member of the American Association for the Advancement of Science, Phi Kappa Phi, and Sigma Xi. In addition to her work in executive management and organization development, she has engaged in research on conformity, dynamics of win-lose conflict, and creative decision making.

Robert R. Blake is chairman of Scientific Methods, Inc. He holds a bachelor's degree in psychology from Berea College

(1940), a master's degree in psychology from the University of Virginia (1941), and a doctoral degree in psychology from the University of Texas at Austin (1947), where he was a professor until 1964. He has lectured at Harvard, Oxford, and Cambridge universities; worked on special extended assignments at the Tavistock Clinic, London, as a Fulbright Scholar. He is a diplomate in Industrial and Organizational Psychology, American Board of Professional Psychology; a fellow of the American Psychological Association; and a member of Phi Kappa Phi, Pi Gamma Mu, and Sigma Xi.

Mouton and Blake have coauthored a series of books, including *The New Managerial Grid* (1964, 1978), *The Secretary Grid* (1983), *Productivity: The Human Side* (1981), and *The Academic Administrator Grid* (1981). They have served as consultants with governments, industries, and universities in forty countries. Among many other assignments, Mouton and Blake have served as consultants to seven of the top ten *Fortune* companies, to the federal government, and to the U.S. Senate on the structure and functioning of presidential commissions.

They also conduct seminars on synergogy for training and development personnel, academics, and educational administrators.

Synergogy

A New Strategy
for Education, Training,
and Development

1

Increasing Learner Motivation
and Involvement

The tempo of change is accelerating, and we are entering an era in which increasingly greater premiums will be attached to effective and efficient educational methods. As our society becomes even more technologically demanding, education and training will reach beyond academic settings into industry, government, professional development programs, and so on. This fact requires that we reassess a major issue in education: how best to enable children, adolescents, and adults to learn what they need to know. At the heart of this issue lies the topic of motivation: unless learners are adequately motivated they will not perform effectively, nor will they find learning rewarding or satisfying.

For some learners, the subject matter itself is inherently motivating and understanding is its own reward. Such cases of "pure" learning, in which the material itself motivates the learner to learn, represent the ideal situation. However, much of what people need to know may not necessarily be rewarding in and of itself but is important for use in practical activities such as programming a computer or understanding a city ordinance concerning plumbing. In these cases the ultimate application may motivate learners, but some will need other sources of motivation as well.

Yet many indicators suggest that our formal education system is failing to motivate students. For example, the high school, college, and university dropout rates suggest that many students experience little or no personal satisfaction as they sit

1

in classrooms. Even for students who stay within the system, absenteeism and discipline are matters of concern. Other evidences of increased disenchantment include cramming as a way, not of learning, but of "beating" the system; the use of ponies to pass a course without understanding it; contracting with outsiders to write theses, dissertations, and term papers; and other strategies for getting through without being involved. Although none of these practices is new, all seem to be more prevalent than they were a few years ago. The irony is that the public demands additional avenues of education. Although this demand is largely being met by community schools, university continuing education departments, and so on, adults are resentful of approaches that do not fulfill their needs.

Our experience and research have led us to conclude that the relative ineffectiveness of current educational and training programs is an inevitable result of the character of the teacher-student relationship in the traditional class or training room. The most customary teacher-student relationship is based on the *pedagogic* model. Here, the teacher, by virtue of knowledge and experience, is an expert in a position of authority over the student. The teacher determines the direction, rate, and character of learning; in short, the teacher "teaches" and the students comply by listening, taking notes, and sometimes asking or answering questions. Although pedagogy allows the efficient delivery of information, it can also induce passivity, apathy, and even active resistance from students. Such attitudes thwart learning and sometimes lead to attendance and discipline problems. In its purest form, pedagogy induces compliance and obedience at the expense of student involvement and responsibility.

Criticisms of pedagogy are not new, but most attempts to replace the conventional teacher-centered model with student-centered approaches have not been successful in stimulating committed learning. Discovery learning, "open classrooms," and progressive approaches such as Summerhill reduce the authority of the teacher but have failed to generate widespread acceptance by teachers or students (Neill, 1960; Nyquist and Hawes, 1972). Similarly, practitioners of adult education have devised *andragogic* methods in which the instructor serves as a facilitator rather than an authority figure. While these methods induce participative involvement (Knowles, 1973; Revans, 1982), the learners still are dependent on the instructor for social context and emotional safety. Thus it seems that the instructional model *itself*—and not necessarily a given teacher's comprehension of a subject, facility in communicating, desire to be helpful, and so on—is at the root of this fundamental problem.

How Authority Can Block Learning

Let us consider why pedagogic and andragogic models are less than fully effective methods for communicating relevant knowledge. To understand this, we must focus on the dynamics of the adult learning years, which begin at the age of twelve or fifteen. Simply put, until an individual attains the maturity of a self-responsible adult, he or she is in the process of moving from dependency to autonomy. During this period a learner can become resentful, sometimes intensely so, of the continuing efforts of teachers to provide direction. At this time the learner is particularly eager to be self-reliant, despite an instructor's misgivings. Some learners soon find their sense of autonomy and self-esteem confirmed through a general situation of responsible self-identity. But for others the struggle to achieve autonomy is far more difficult and may not be completed until middle age or later.

It is important to emphasize that these individual struggles to achieve autonomy reflect societal conditions; they are not biologically or developmentally inevitable. This conclusion has been well established by anthropological research concerning societies in which the transition from child to full adult status is completed by a ritual that follows a period of learning (Mead, 1949).

The period of transition to full mature adult status in American society has two important characteristics that are relevant to learning: authority repudiation and colleague affiliation. The intensity with which any individual manifests these characteristics varies, but the prevalence of these responses in modern industrialized cultures accounts for the ineffectiveness of the authority-obedience model of learning.

Authority repudiation is a strong term to use, yet it is an apt description that denotes the individual's rejection of supervision, direction, instruction, and so on. In general, individuals who are struggling to assert their autonomy tend to resist the efforts of persons in authority to exercise control over them. The authority may be a parent, a police officer, an instructor, or a boss. The individual does not necessarily reject the *legitimacy* of the authority, but rather seeks to extend his or her own autonomy by working to control the interaction with the authority.

This relationship between dependent individuals and authority figures was perhaps first systematically examined by Freud. From his psychoanalytic work he concluded that therapeutic help is unlikely to be beneficial unless the patient first establishes a positive, accepting, and basically dependent relationship with the therapist. During the course of therapy, however, the patient's attitude shifts to a negative and often antagonistic orientation toward the therapist. Thereafter, the therapist aids the patient to comprehend the motivations that underlie both blind dependence and intense rejection. Freud thought that through this three-phase process, individuals could be helped to overcome barriers to autonomy.

At the same time that the individual is resisting authority figures as sources of direction, colleagues are becoming a much more important source of mutual reliance. In adolescence, sexual interests unfold, friendships blossom, confidante relationships are established, groups and cliques form, and experiences of intimacy are shared. As a result, teenagers are drawn together as people who can share and understand one another within their own subculture, whose standards are their own rather than outsiders'. Teenagers are open to one another and very much influenced by how their peers view them. This openness to colleague influence usually continues, though in a more subdued form, into adulthood.

In addition, teenagers share essentially the same pursuit of autonomy. Each tends to rely on contemporaries as models for self-direction. A teenager who continues to lean on author-ity figures is likely to be rejected by contemporaries as imma-ture or childish. Within their groups, teenagers can vent their hostile feelings toward authority figures, who become "anti-models." Such colleague affiliation dynamics bear directly on students' responses to the authority-obedience model in the classroom. For example, one way by which a teenager can gain colleague approval is to challenge a teacher. Another way is to object to the slightest token of arbitrariness or unfairness on the part of authorities, and to get others to rally around in demand-ing justice from the teacher or administrative personnel.

Thus we see why the traditional pedagogic model evokes passivity, resentment, and even hostility from learners. As long as teachers define their task as telling students what to learn, how to learn, and when to learn, they are likely both to impair students' motivation and to perpetuate the pattern of depen-dency.

Colleague-Oriented Learning

If, however, educators can create conditions that shift the responsibility for learning from the teacher to the students, then there is no authority figure for students to rebel against. Furthermore students' developing colleague affiliations can be used to work toward, rather than against, learning. Finally, methods that shift the responsibility to learners can be used with adult learners as well as school or college students.

To what degree is it possible to promote such a shift of responsibility? Evidence comes from a number of fields, some of which are quite remote from the classroom, and is docu-mented in clinical work, field studies, and experimental para-digms (Riessman, 1965). In all these cases, the learning ap-proach is based on having peers or colleagues teach one another.

For example, other things being equal, dry alcoholics in a group are as well or better able to help other alcoholics to learn to control their behavior than are psychiatrists, ministers, or other counselors (*Alcoholics Anonymous,* 1955). Working to-gether, former drug addicts are equally or more effective in as-sisting drug addicts to learn to solve their problems than medical personnel, psychiatrists, or ministers (Enright, 1971). Ghetto residents who have succeeded in commercial, educational, and similar social endeavors are equally or more effective in helping other ghetto residents break out of the poverty cycle than are ministers or social workers (Hallowitz, 1968). Individuals who have themselves been prone to neurotic reactions are sometimes as capable of helping one another gain insight into neurotic reactions as are psychologists and psychiatrists (Low, 1966).

Programs for adult literacy development have an equal or a more favorable result when taught by persons who share the learners' cultural heritage yet who have overcome illiteracy, than when taught by experts for whom literacy has not been a problem since early childhood (Laubach and Laubach, 1960). Industrial education experiments and academic experiments similarly demonstrate that students can tutor other students with results that are equal to or better than those achieved by instructors (Gartner, Kohler, and Riessman, 1971).

These diverse reports all suggest that peers and colleagues can effectively help one another to learn, that identification between learners and their peer teachers provides support and motivation for learning. The learning blockages traceable to the teacher-tell model can be avoided by learning situations that make the fullest possible use of colleague-affiliation dynamics.

But colleague-oriented learning seems impossible if all the students are equally uninformed, for how can students help one another learn if none of them knows the subject? In the effort to transfer responsibility to students, the teacher cannot simply abandon students to their own insufficient resources. As critics of "progressive education," "open classrooms," and "discovery" learning have observed, although the resulting student involvement in learning situations may be high, the actual learning achieved may be minimal.

Synergogic Learning Designs

Synergogic learning designs offer an important strategy for obviating such problems. A learning design is a set of instructions and instruments that directs students' colleague-oriented learning. A detailed rationale for the four synergogic designs is presented in Chapter Two, and the designs themselves in Chapters Three through Six. At this point, the designs are briefly introduced in comparison with more-traditional approaches to three aspects of learning: comprehending *knowledge,* such as facts, data, logic, principles, and generalizations; acquisition of conceptual and mechanical *skills*; and the development of *attitudes, values,* and *beliefs.*

Knowledge

Acquiring and integrating facts, and learning and applying principles are probably the most common activities in high school and university classrooms as well as in on-the-job business education. Two synergogic designs, the Team Effectiveness Design (TED) and the Team-Member Teaching Design (TMTD), enable students to work together to learn facts and principles. Unlike the pedagogic model, these designs permit learners to work in the absence of an authority or expert. Unlike open classrooms or discovery approaches, the designs provide guidance and direction for the learning teams.

Skills

Of the many approaches currently employed in helping learners acquire a skill, the two widely used are behavior modification and coaching. In the *behavior modification* approach the teacher or trainer reinforces the desired responses to increase the likelihood of their recurring and becoming either habitual or part of the learner's available repertoire that can be produced at will. Unwanted responses are ignored or actively discouraged, so that their repetition will decrease and eventually be extinguished.

In a *coaching* model an expert, someone with already perfected skills, outlines to a novice the steps to be implemented. The expert critiques the effectiveness at critical points to stimulate repetition on a "practice makes perfect" basis. Behavioral reinforcements may also be used to facilitate learning. This is, in effect, a tutoring situation when the interaction is one-to-one, but it can approach the conditions of the traditional classroom when the coach-learner ratio is one-to-fifteen or one-to-thirty.

The third synergogic design, the Performance Judging Design (PJD), is intended to help learners acquire and perfect skills in colleague teams that develop criteria for performance and use these criteria to critique one another's skills—again in the absence of an authority or expert.

Attitudes

One of the most neglected aspects of contemporary education is the significant influence attitudes have on learning and performance. Administrators of companies, universities, and schools, as well as teachers, usually pause to consider the quality of employees' or students' attitudes only when they have become so negative or deviant as to result in confused, divisive, unacceptable, or even illegal behavior. Other attitudes are likely to be regarded as a personal and individual matter—part of one's personality—and are rarely seen as subject matter that is significant enough to be brought into focus through teaching, evaluation, or appraisal.

In many respects—and specifically in private areas of life —such reticence to intervene in others' attitudes is appropriate and valid. In democratic societies, for example, no responsible educator or trainer would prescribe attitudes toward politics, religion, or issues of private morality. Nor is it relevant to view such attitudes as aspects of on-the-job efficiency or as career-advancement criteria. A corporate president has no claim on the political or religious values of executives, supervisors, and other employees.

However, certain attitudes do affect student or employee performance, satisfaction, and development. Positive attitudes can strongly motivate an individual to apply knowledge or skills to constructive purposes, while negative attitudes can hinder the appropriate use of the knowledge or skills. Aiding individuals to test their attitudes against criteria, to become better aware of how their attitudes influence their thought and behavior, to perceive a range of available attitudes—all can serve a vital educational purpose. The fourth synergogic design, the Clarifying Attitudes Design (CAD), is used to enable learners to study and articulate their own attitudes.

Synergogy as an Alternative

Synergogy provides an alternative to both pedagogy and andragogy, seeking to avoid the weaknesses of both: the role of authority in pedagogic settings and the excessive reliance on the student already knowing what he or she needs to know in andragogic settings. At the same time synergogy preserves the strengths of these two approaches: the role of the expert in providing authoritative subject matter (in the form of learning designs) about the topic to be studied and the proactive involvement of the learner in being responsible for learning.

Synergogy thus provides a systematic framework for approaching the problems encountered in education, training, and development. Its four fundamental differences from other approaches involve: (1) replacing authority figures with learning designs and instruments managed by a learning administrator; (2) enabling learners to become proactive participants who exercise responsibility for their own learning; (3) applying to education the concept of *synergy*, in which the learning gain that results from teamwork exceeds the gain made by individuals learning alone; and (4) using learners' colleague affiliations to provide motivation for learning. Specific sources of social motivation include each learner's desire to increase his or her personal effectiveness and effectiveness as a team member, to collaborate with and gain approval from one's colleagues, to participate in order to increase the likelihood of team success and to exercise personal autonomy in learning.

The mention of *motivation* returns us to the starting point of this chapter: effective learning requires that the learners be motivated. Synergogy presents designs for organizing learning environments so as to avoid conditions that decrease motivations for learning and to provide situations that reinforce individuals' desire to learn by helping one another.

2

Principles and Designs
for Enhancing Learning

ഔᕲᕲ   The concept of learner-centered education has had a long history of illustrious advocates. Yet efforts to translate this idea into educational practice have usually been met by resistance, which has in turn only strengthened the hold of instructor-centered education. Why has the sound concept of learner-centered education failed to become the primary mode of education, training, and development? One explanation is that when teachers have attempted to extend responsibility for learning to the learners, they have not done so in ways that resulted in improved educational outcomes. Parents, city and state government, federal agencies, as well as industrial managers responsible for funding instruction, felt that educational achievement was being sacrificed to irresponsible permissiveness.

Synergogy differs from other learner-centered methodologies in positing three basic principles that promote educational success. First, synergogy offers learners meaningful direction in the form of learning designs and learning instruments. A learning design is a format that structures the process of learning by providing a framework of orderly steps for acquiring knowledge, attitudes, or skills. The design is presented through learning instruments, tactical instructions that enable the learner to learn without a teacher; such instruments include a variety of materials: true-false or multiple-choice tests, case studies, descriptions of dilemmas, text material, evaluation procedures, and the like. Learning instruments thus supply the guidance and

10

direction usually provided by an instructor. But learning instruments do not provoke resistance to authority or dependency responses from learners, problems that typically interfere with teacher-student relationships. The instrument is neutral, a set of written instructions whose value is established by its utility.

Learning designs and instruments are also superior to various other forms of providing direction, such as the competency models and behavioral objectives used in self-directed learning, criterion-referenced learning, and so on. While these methods do provide direction, they tend to promote the learners' continuing dependency on the expert or to prevent learners from developing their own sense of responsibility. For example, by presenting learners with a competency model and the opportunity to validate that model, an instructor may help students develop a sense of ownership, but the model in fact often belongs to the teacher.

Second, synergogy relies on teamwork, rather than on individual or group work, to enhance learners' involvement and participation. That members of a group can learn from one another is widely acknowledged. But not every group is necessarily supportive of socially constructive learning; some groups function as social environments that support destructive norms and behaviors. For this reason, synergogic learning designs distinguish between a group and a learning team. A learning team is a group that has explicit goals and objectives, tasks, procedures, and measured operational outcomes of its effectiveness. Among the team's procedures are methods for resolving or avoiding problems that often plague groups—for example, disagreements as to the nature of the task, interpersonal antagonisms or rivalries, detours caused by irrelevancies, and so on. Team effectiveness results from the members' acquiring skills in solving these problems and their having a framework in which such problems are less likely to occur.

The third principle essential to synergogic methods is that of synergy, the concept that under certain conditions the whole can be more than the sum of its parts. In the traditional discussion group, each member may benefit from his or her participation but not necessarily at a level commensurate with that individual's full potential. In contrast, the synergogic team uses learning designs and learning instruments that allow members to methodically share their knowledge, explore one another's reasoning, and examine implications for correct understanding. As a result, participants achieve a greater level of understanding than they otherwise would have.

In sum, synergogic methods offer learners professional or expert guidance in the form of learning instruments and designs. Learners assume initiative and responsibility through reliance on colleague teams that avoid the undesirable consequences of poorly structured group activity. Team interactions as regulated by the learning designs provide the essential structure that permits individuals to achieve synergistic gains while maintaining responsibility and control of the learning process.

Benefits and Advantages

The benefits and advantages of synergogy are numerous, as attested to by the method's growing popularity in secondary, postsecondary, and adult education. The principal benefit is that the synergogic method produces significant educational outcomes. There are several reasons for synergogy's effectiveness as a learning method. Probably the most important is that synergogy places responsibility for learning on the learners and therefore stimulates them to use their personal resources in constructive ways to help one another. Almost of equal importance is that synergogic learning is fun. The spirit of competition that arises among learning teams is as enjoyable as any game of organized sport. Third, synergogy stimulates individuals' motivations to contribute and to accept the contributions of others, for only in this way is it possible for everyone to learn; a commitment to the team stimulates individuals to do their best, as well as to help one another. Fourth, learning teams operate under their own guidance, without a formal instructor to supervise or direct them. As a result, teams find themselves grappling with managing time, resolving differences between members, and facing other real-life choices and responsibilities. The challenge of being effective is very real, and the increased reward of success great. Finally, the method's clear measures of performance enable learners to observe their progress and prompt them to achieve ever-higher scores.

Other, more specific benefits of synergogy include the following:

1. Broad applicability:
   - Synergogy is applicable to all forms of learning, whether the material to be studied concerns knowledge, attitudes, or skills.
   - Synergogy can be constructively used by learners from ten to twelve years of age and older.
   - Synergogy does not require learners to be able to read; the material to be learned can be presented on video or audio cassettes or by means of other visual aids.
2. Modest resources:
   - Synergogic teams do not need elaborate physical facilities, only chairs, tables, and a blackboard or flip chart.
   - Synergogic methods place no significant limitations on class size because the size of the learning team (not the student-teacher ratio) is the significant factor. Thus a class can be as large as the meeting space available.
   - Synergogic teams do not require the presence of experts in the subject matter under study. Such experts make their contribution in the preparation of the learning instruments, which can be reproduced and used by teams working alone or in the presence of a learner administrator. This process is particularly important in developing countries where educator resources are scarce.
   - Once a design and instruments are standardized, they can be reused unless changes in the subject matter necessitate updating or revision.
3. Increased learning and secondary learning:
   - Team groupings can be homogeneous or heterogeneous, as needed to promote self-paced learning and meaningful competition.
   - Synergogy produces secondary learning gains: as team members develop their interaction skills, they become

more socially competent individuals. Similarly as team members discipline one another, they develop a mature sense of responsibility.

- Team review of members' individual performance enables individuals to identify and rectify misunderstandings.
- Teamwork in spotting mistakes or misunderstandings permits team members to learn without feeling downgraded by an expert or formal authority figure.
- The designs promote cooperation and reduce individual competitiveness; even though individual learning may occur when a team's performance is not successful, greater learning can be expected when the team does well.

Limitations

One major limitation in the use of synergogy results from educators' attitudes toward learner-centered methods. Some instructors, for example, feel uncomfortable with learning designs that enable students to turn to one another rather than to the instructor. Instructors trained in traditional instructor-centered pedagogic or andragogic approaches may initially feel threatened by synergogic methods, fearing that such methods might render their expertise and teaching or facilitator skills useless. But any initial discomfort or uncertainty can be allayed. An understanding of the principles and beneficial outcomes of synergogic methods should demonstrate to instructors that synergogy enables them to use their expertise in writing and designing materials and instruments that will be widely used. And instructors can then use their pedagogic or andragogic skills in situations in which such approaches are best suited: teaching highly technical subjects to learners of established competence, conducting seminars for graduate students or other preprofessionals, and instructing others who are engaged in inquiries that are not programmatic.

A second limitation that restricts the use of synergogy results from students' attitudes toward extrinsic rewards. In pedagogic methods, the instructor provides such rewards as positive remarks on an exam or paper, high grades, or a pleasant smile and a word of encouragement. Such extrinsic rewards are also often present, but to a lesser degree, in the andragogic setting. Synergogy largely precludes any such rewards because the learning designs and instruments eliminate the role of instructor as authority figure. Thus synergogy is sometimes disappointing for students who derive satisfaction from extrinsic rewards granted by authority figures. While their disappointment arises from values embedded within traditional academic culture independent of the validity of the fundamental assumptions of synergogy, nonetheless, students who want to have a dependent relationship with an authority figure are likely to remain unsatisfied with synergogic approaches.

The third limitation derives from the need to create designs and instruments of high quality. The requisite skills include the writing and preparation of manuscripts, multiple-choice tests, explicit rationales, attitude questionnaires, and so on. None of these tasks require any unusual abilities, but instructors with little or no experience in designing instruments may be unwilling to take the time to learn to do these tasks well. However, interested persons can learn much from this book. In addition, technical documents about test construction, measurement, and evaluation (such as textbooks used in colleges of education) can be consulted, and seminars that provide a hands-on experience in designing and using instruments according to synergogic learning assumptions are available.*

Tactics: The Four Designs

In Chapter One we differentiated three major forms of learning: the acquisition of knowledge, the enhancement of attitudes, and the development of skills. In general terms, *knowl-*

---

*Information can be obtained from the Synergogy Network, P.O. Box 195, Austin, Texas 78767. This network provides informal linkages between people engaged in or wanting further information about this approach to education, training, and development.

edge comprises facts, principles, theorems, propositions, and the like; *attitudes* are patterns of individual responses that reflect values, judgment, and feelings; and *skills* concern the ability to perform some set of operations in a competent manner.

Success in most activities requires a combination of adequate knowledge, positive attitudes, and some degree of skill. For example, driving an automobile involves knowledge of the rules of the road, and at least basic knowledge of the operating principles of the equipment (fuel, cooling, lubrication, and so on). Relevant attitudes include risk-taking or conservative behavior that affects safety practices, such as dimming lights. Among the necessary skills are steering, shifting gears, and parallel parking. In the actual practice of driving, of course, knowledge, attitudes, and skills interact. But for learning purposes they can be separated and dealt with one at a time.

Synergogic methods can be applied to each of these three forms of learning. In this section we present an overview of the four principal synergogic designs. Two are related to acquiring knowledge; the third pertains to developing skills; and the fourth concerns the learners' self-awareness and development of attitudes. More specific discussion of the four basic designs are presented in Chapters Three through Six. To permit comparisons between the designs, these chapters follow a uniform outline. First, an overview of each design is presented to give a broad orientation to the entire sequence. The learning materials needed to implement the design are then presented in detail under the heading "Design Preparation." It is important to note, however, that these preparatory tasks may be divided between a subject-matter expert and a learning administrator.

The subsequent step-by-step examination of the various segments of each design sequence include sample instructions and administrative considerations of implementation. Case examples illustrate specific applications of each design. These excerpts from learning instruments and instructions highlight significant features of the designs but, to avoid repetition, they do not always cover all steps of the design. Each chapter concludes with suggested variations of the design, a summary of its strengths and limitations, and examples of applications in a variety of settings.

Team Effectiveness Design (TED)

In the Team Effectiveness Design, each of a team's learners assesses his or her knowledge prior to team discussion. After an initial review (prestudy) of the material to be learned, each learner completes a given set of true-false or multiple-choice questions. The team members then work together to reach consensus on the best answer to each test question. Members present their choices and reasons for them and learn about other members' choices. Since the task is to achieve consensus, participants have the opportunity to exchange information, to explain their reasoning, to assess the reasons and evidence provided by others, and to use logic in weighing the pros and cons of each alternative as the best answer. Later, in general sessions, objective scoring enables team members to assess their individual work, and the team's consensus answers are scored for comparison with other teams. The answer key also provides a rationale for each answer, which further aids team members in understanding why each correct answer, according to the key, is regarded as the most valid. Team members then use an evaluation period to assess how well they worked as a team and to plan how to increase their effectiveness. Of particular interest are those cases in which one member offered the correct answer but was unable to achieve team consensus for that answer. Open and highly involving discussions usually result from team members' analyzing why they did not agree on the correct answer when it was proposed.

A distinguishing feature of this design is that it calls for mutual responsibility among a team of learners. The learning instruments present the subject matter to be learned. If a person who otherwise serves as an instructor is present, his or her role is not to present the subject matter but to administer the instruments and to help students manage their own learning processes. Yet, in contrast to discovery learning or open classroom, professional responsibility for the subject matter is retained in the construction of the instruments.

The TED is useful for presenting subject matter that requires students to learn facts and data and to deduce principles or consequences. The learner's interest in the subject matter is supported by his or her inherent curiosity about how and why others think as they do. Additional motivation may derive from a learner's desire to interest or even impress other team members through personal contributions to the discussion.

Team-Member Teaching Design (TMTD)

In the Team-Member Teaching Design, participants are responsible for learning an assigned portion of the subject matter and teaching it to the others. Once each member's part is fitted with the others, the entire body of knowledge is known to all. Thus, the TMTD somewhat resembles a jigsaw puzzle. At the beginning, all the parts are present but unassembled. The learning design provides the structure by which the parts can be put together so that the whole picture is visible and each participant understands it. (Team-member teaching, in which the teaching is done by a team's members, is not to be confused with team teaching, in which two or more instructors share responsibility for a group of students.)

This design requires that the subject matter be subdivided and a part assigned as prestudy to each member. When the team assembles, the member with the first part teaches that material to the others; then other members in turn teach their parts. A comprehensive test of the material is administered to assess each participant's understanding. The answer key provides the expert rationale for each item and helps learners understand whatever questions each may have missed. In a subsequent brief critique period, team members assess how well each seems to have learned and communicated the assigned subject matter, and members suggest how individuals could increase their effectiveness.

This design stimulates learners to study and become experts on their assigned portion because only such mastery will enable them to help their team. Similarly, the team members being taught are highly motivated to help the presenter impart what he or she studied as prework.

Like the TED, TMTD is most useful for aiding the learners to acquire information, facts, and data. The TMTD is particularly appropriate for training managers, salespeople, and others for whom presentation skills in communicating knowledge and information are important. In addition, this design fosters participants' listening skills and abilities to pose constructive questions in response to others' presentations of information. The TMTD demands of the team members different study skills than the TED: members preparing for team-member teaching are more likely to study in depth and need to synthesize the information so as to present it logically and coherently. Thus members' learning is facilitated by their having to organize an informative presentation. The TMTD and TED can be used in combination to add variety to the learning situation.

Performance Judging Design (PJD)

The Performance Judging Design is a useful approach for classes in which learners are to acquire practical skills. In industry and commerce, for example, applications of this design include training in operating a machine set-up, conducting various kinds of interviews, or writing an effective business letter or technical report. Noncommercial applications include instruction in playing a musical instrument or public speaking.

This design is intended to help learners exercise individual responsibility for their team members' skill development. First, participants develop the effectiveness criteria that apply in performing a particular skill. These criteria enable learners to judge the quality of their own performance so that they need not rely on others to evaluate the soundness of that performance. When learners have an explicit understanding of the criteria, they can also monitor their performance outside the learning situation.

Second, each person produces initial evidence of his or her skill level, which can then be compared with the levels achieved by others and which can be judged by the learners themselves in terms of the previously established criteria. Individuals also receive colleague critiques of their product or performance. By acting on these specific suggestions, learners are likely to reach a level of effectiveness that satisfies the criteria.

Clarifying Attitudes Design (CAD)

People's attitudes profoundly influence their effectiveness as well as personal satisfaction, and attitudes are a significant aspect of social emotional learning. Nonetheless, many people regard attitudes as private affairs that are not a legitimate part of education. Although the coercive manipulation of personal attitudes has no place in education, generally it is helpful for people to freely explore their attitudes, to gain insight and enlightened self-control, and to discover how their attitudes may limit or distort the scope or quality of their performance.

The first phase of the Clarifying Attitudes Design helps learners assess their attitudes through a sentence-completion item or bipolar attitude scale. Then learners assemble to identify and discuss the position on the attitude scale that they agree is the soundest in the light of available information and known circumstances. Each individual then repeats the prework items in order to assess whether his or her attitudes have changed as a result of the discussion. In the critique period learners evaluate the implications of whatever attitude changes have occurred and develop generalizations as to the implications for their own performance.

This design thus enables learners to discover whether their attitudes have a sound basis in available facts, data, and logic. Just as unfounded negative attitudes develop into unreasoned prejudices, so can unfounded positive attitudes yield an optimism that does not lead to constructive joint action. Similarly, learners may discover that they were unaware of having a particular attitude toward some matter or unaware of alternative attitudes that might be embraced.

This design also provides participants with an opportunity to hear a variety of opinions. Because most people tend to associate with others who are like-minded, certain attitudes tend to be reinforced within everyday interactions. But the CAD motivates learners to examine their attitudes and test their validity in terms of available information and new alternatives. Learners thus discover what their attitudes are and come to recognize the similarities and differences with attitudes held by others and the reasons for them. The approach to comparison learning applied to subjective processes is often experienced by learners as freeing them from constraints they previously had not recognized.

Table 1 provides examples of subjects appropriate to each of the four designs.

Table 1. Synergogic Designs and Sample Subject Matter.

General Subject	TED or TMTD (Knowledge Acquisition)	PJD (Skill Development)	CAD (Attitude Study)
Computers	Tasks that can be performed by a word processing system.	Writing reports on a word processor	Management's attitudes toward the computerized office and their effect on productivity
Leadership	Comparative study of management's philosophy of leadership in Japanese and American corporations	Exercising authority and leadership in the office	Styles of leadership that provoke antiauthoritarian noncompliance
Firefighting	Characteristics of the four major types of fires	Techniques for fighting each of the four major types of fires	Fears about fires and overcoming them
Modern Architecture	Principal styles of modern architecture	Drawing blueprints and visualizing them in three dimensions	Design factors that promote public use of malls and plazas
Multiple-Choice Test Construction	Theories of testing and the statistical validity of multiple-choice tests	Constructing a test for junior high school algebra classes	Student views of multiple-choice tests: learning experience or anxiety-producing torment?

3

ഗ ᏻᏬᏭᏮᏬᏭᏮᏬ ᏭᏮ

Acquiring Knowledge
Through Mutual Deliberation

The Team Effectiveness
Design (TED)

ഗ ᏻᏬ Team Effectiveness Designs are based on two main premises. The first is simply that two heads or more are better than one because each person can explain to the others what he or she knows, and all can learn from one another. The second premise is that learners, at least those from age ten through the late adult years, find the active participation in shared learning to be very motivating.

Overview of the Design

Segment 1: Individual preparation by learners
Segment 2: Teamwork
   Discussions to reach agreement
   Scoring of individual and team answers
Segment 3: Interpretation of scores
Segment 4: Critique of teamwork
Segment 5: Evaluation of individual progress

In preparation for implementing the design, the designer must prepare the learning instruments, that is, the prework assignment (either a reading assignment or an audiovisual presen-

22

tation) and a multiple-choice test. The learners must be divided into teams—a class of thirty-five, for example, becomes a set of seven teams with five members each.

Each learner then individually completes the prework assignment and the test (segment 1). Learners are thus prepared to discuss the subject matter in learning teams (segment 2). In the learning team the first task is to achieve a set of agreed-on answers to the same test questions. Scoring of individual prework and the team performance is followed by a team discussion of the rationale for correct and incorrect answers and an examination of why some questions were missed and others answered correctly (segment 3). Critique of the interaction process and evaluation of each learner's progress complete the activity (segments 4 and 5). Descriptions of each segment follow the section on design preparation. As noted in Chapter Two, this preparation may be divided between a subject-matter expert and a learning administrator.

Design Preparation

Whatever material is to be learned is usually presented to the teams in the form of a manuscript or text that contains the relevant principles, theorems, facts, information, or data. The text is followed by questions that cover the content. These questions are usually in multiple-choice form, although true-false or other forms can be used. Two versions of the questionnaire can be constructed so that one can be used in the learning design itself and the other employed later as a postmeasure of individual comprehension.

Multiple-choice items that require the learner to apply the material in some way, such as by drawing conclusions or inferences from a previously presented principle are preferable to items that can be answered by merely locating the information in the text. Questions that include plausible but invalid answers are useful in aiding the learner to sort out what is actually true from pat answers that may look good but are incorrect. Thus the questionnaire should be constructed so that the greatest likelihood of getting a good score comes from listening, thinking through, arguing, weighing evidence, and so on. Answering such questions is intrinsically rewarding as most people enjoy a battle of wits.

The best instrument for learning purposes is a measure that learners find to be of moderate difficulty, that is, one on which about half the questions are correctly answered during the individual prework. If the test is too hard no one is likely to be able to find the answer, but if it is too easy there is no discussion because everyone knows the answer.

Developing a Multiple-Choice Test

With the following sequence of steps as a guideline, a designer can compose a multiple-choice test for a particular manuscript or text.

Identify a learning segment. Identify the portion of the manuscript or text to be covered by the test. Such a segment should address a single topic in a coherent way. For a two-hour teamwork session, the segment should probably be no more than fifty pages. However, a designer should exercise personal judgment in this area. The actual number of pages that can be handled by students is a function of their educational level, the amount of prework or preparatory time, relative density and complexity of the material, and so on.

Identify key concepts. Review the text to identify the key points contained in the manuscript. Key points are those deemed essential to the students' overall understanding and comprehension of the subject matter, and these key points will be the focus of the test questions. Merely because a particular point suggests an easily written question is no justification for testing on that point. Rather, the questions should be strategically distributed according to the key points in the subject matter.

Decide on the number of items. The number of items should be determined by the number of key knowledge points in the manuscript. For a two-hour teamwork session, no more than forty questions should be offered when the items are of moderate difficulty. Because team members with less experience are unlikely to be as effective in terms of interaction skills or to inquire as deeply of one another as those with more experience, no correction is needed for team experience.

Prepare item stems. The *stem* of an item is the opening statement that precedes the sentence-completion alternatives. The stem should have as much pertinent question-orienting information as possible while being concise and crisp. The stem must also be in a form that will allow the alternative answers to be concise. The following example illustrates a poorly constructed question: both the stem and alternatives are so complex that the reader easily forgets the content of alternative A by the time he or she reaches alternative C.

It has been stated that (1) there are four major purposes of team building and that (2) there is an optimal priority concerning the order of implementing these four purposes with organizational teams. The optimal order is which of the following?

A. Establishing and/or clarifying goals and objectives; establishing and/or clarifying roles and responsibilities; establishing and/or clarifying policies and procedures; improving human relationships.

B. Establishing and/or clarifying roles and responsibilities; establishing and/or clarifying goals and objectives; establishing and/or clarifying policies and procedures; improving human relationships.

C. Establishing and/or clarifying policies and procedures; establishing and/or clarifying goals and objectives; improving human relationships; establishing and/or clarifying roles and responsibilities.

D. Improving human relationships; establishing and/or clarifying policies and procedures; establishing and/or clarifying goals and objectives; establishing and/or clarifying roles and responsibilities.

In contrast, the following question is soundly constructed. The stem is straightforward and the alternatives thought-provoking but clear.

The use of an instrument in synergogic learning designs is to:
A. Influence people to place value on teamwork.
B. Create a colleague learning environment around a common task.
C. Set up an experimental situation for members to role play solutions to interpersonal problems.
D. Bring scientific insight to bear upon the problems of working in teams.
E. Provide a programmed learning experience of human interaction.

In writing stems and alternatives, one should avoid taking easily remembered words or phrases directly from the text as these might prompt a correct response despite a learner's faulty comprehension of all the issues entailed.

Write alternative answers. The number of alternative sentence-completion answers to each question stem can be as few as two—true-false—or as many as four or five. (Questions with more than five alternatives are both time-consuming and likely to require discriminations so subtle as to result in poor performance.) The number of alternatives per question should reflect the amount of time available to learners for completing and discussing the questionnaire and the fineness of differentiation that students need make in order to adequately understand the material. Generally, the more thorough the degree of understanding needed, the more desirable it becomes to provide a larger number of choices.

Each question stem and its alternative answers should be drafted on separate sheets of paper or on cards. Write the correct answer first and identify it with a check mark. If one or two "distractor" alternatives immediately suggest themselves, write those down. Continue to write stems, leaving the writing of a full set of alternatives for each stem until later. It is usually easier to come back and complete all the distractor alternatives than to write them question by question. After writing down and editing all the stems and their correct answers, one can always adopt a purposely "distracting" frame of mind and develop the remaining incorrect alternatives. Incorrect alternatives can also be elicited from a sample group of learners. Simply give them the stems and ask them to complete the items.

The distractor alternatives should be sufficiently plausible as to mislead, by their apparent rightness, a student who either has not studied the material sufficiently well, or who, for any other reason, does not comprehend the key point that is being tested by the question. Of course, the false alternative that one student might immediately reject could still be a significant distractor to another. And a subtle false alternative is likely to cause more trouble for a well-prepared and discerning student than for someone who is making hasty choices. Thus, in general, it is good to have a near-miss false alternative, but only if the rationale for its being incorrect can be clearly and fully comprehended by a discriminating student. Avoid offering wild alternatives that are obviously implausible or invalid. Strive for alternatives that will enable students to learn something in the process of rejecting incorrect ones. Both trickery and triviality should also be avoided. Trivial alternatives only cause people to waste time, and trick questions or answers do not measure real knowledge or understanding.

Edit and revise the questionnaire. Review all stems and alternatives and revise as follows:

- The false alternatives and correct answer should be roughly equal in length. Avoid placing lengthy provisos in the correct answer to ensure its precision; the length of the alternatives should not provide clues as to their correctness. Variations that increase the overall challenge of the alternatives are possible in five alternative questions. For example, there can be balanced pairs of longer and shorter distractors, or a long correct answer can be paired with long false alternatives.
- Verify that questions cannot be correctly answered by un-

prepared learners on the basis of pure logic or common sense. Indeed, some of the incorrect answers can be phrased to appeal to common sense and thereby allow learners to discover whether they actually understand the material. Similarly, incorrect choices based on attitudes as contrasted with the facts contained in the document require learners to distinguish between their opinions and facts.

- Reword questions to avoid the use of absolutes such as *always, never, all, none*; such terms have restricted application in the real world as perceived by mature adults. If possible, reword questions that are stated in a negative form; the decoding of a negative question is time-consuming and often produces a confusion unrelated to the learner's understanding of the subject matter.

- Arrange items in a thoughtful order: either following the sequence of the text or in increasing order of difficulty. The first arrangement helps learners perceive the logical flow of the material; the second arrangement allows learners to build their confidence and offers the teams increased success and effectiveness in discussion. Random sequences of questions offer no particular advantage and should be avoided.

- The number of alternatives need not be the same for every item. From three to five alternatives should be offered, depending on the complexity of the subject. If only three alternatives seem appropriate, do not add a fourth simply for symmetry. If each of five alternatives communicates an important point—that is, the rejection of each false alternative is instructive—include all five.

- The correct answers should not appear in any predictable pattern. The use of a table of random numbers will ensure that the placement of the correct alternative (for example, in a five-choice item, whether at A, B, C, D, or E) is completely unpredictable. If such a table is unavailable, review the questionnaire and rearrange correct answers and distractors as randomly as possible.

Pretest the items. If at all possible, pretest the items by asking interested colleagues to read the document, answer the questionnaire, and keep notes that explain their thinking in selecting the correct answer and rejecting the alternatives.

Create an answer key and rationale. Prepare the test in its final form and doublecheck the answer key for accuracy. If possible, the key should include a page reference for each correct answer so that test-takers can locate where the topic was discussed and restudy points they missed.

Creating Teams

Teams may be either homogeneous or heterogeneous in terms of the sex, age, level of competence, level in a work hierarchy or unit, and so on. For planning heterogeneous groups, one may use any random scheme such that different characteristics are equally represented in each team. Randomly constituted teams have no advantage over one another as related to members' initial experience, competence, job experience, technical background, educational level, age, and so on. A planned random method of team composition should thus evenly apportion whatever distinctive characteristics might affect the results.

Other possibilities for creating teams include asking participants to select others with whom they would like to study or sociometric choosing, in which participants' written choices for teammates are used by the learning administrator to compose teams.

Implementing the Design

Segment 1: Individual Preparation by Learners

The manuscript is distributed to the learners for individual study. Working alone, each learner completes the questionnaire. If the test questions demand more than simple factual recall, learners may consult the text while answering the questions. Such review of the text both motivates learners and permits them to refine their understanding of the manuscript.

Segment 2: Teamwork

Discussions to reach agreement. When team members
meet they are given the following instructions: Using the questionnaire each of you completed as prework, teams are to discuss the questions and arrive at an agreement about the most
valid answer to each question. The criterion of validity is that
the answer correspond most closely to what the manuscript
contained or implied. Do not consult the manuscript itself during your discussion.

The teams are also given a time limit. The optimal time
for team discussion for thirty to forty questions is about two
hours, depending, of course, on item difficulty, quality of individuals' preparation, and team size. Additional procedural suggestions may be given, depending on the interaction skills of
team members. For example, the teams may be told to begin by
having each member give his or her answer to the first question
and the reasons for it. Only then does the team discuss the question and seek agreement on the best answer. Teams may also
need suggestions on how to resolve an impasse. They could be
advised to set aside any disputed items until as many agreements as possible have been reached and to then return to the
disputed items for further exploration of members' reasoning
and a renewed effort to resolve differences. In resolving dis-
putes, teams should remember the difference between such
statements as "I disagree with that" and "You are wrong." The
former is neutral with respect to personal acceptance or rejection, while the latter can arouse defensive responses that hinder
cooperation and learning. Teams should also be reminded that a
consensus is an agreement by all members based on reasoning
and understanding, and that although a majority vote may be
necessary to secure agreement it is not desirable.

When instructions such as these are provided, most teams
can function effectively without any one member being designated as leader. This is particularly so after learners have had
the opportunity to use instrumented learning designs and to acquire increased skills of teamwork and cooperation. When there
is no designated leader, each member is likely to be self-regulat-

ing and to feel more responsibility for the effectiveness of the team effort.

Scoring of individual and team answers. When the time for discussion has ended, the answer key is distributed. Both individual answers from prework and the team agreement answers are scored by the learners, with each scoring his or her individual work. Scoring of the team's answers can be completed by the members together or by whichever member finishes first. By sharing the scoring, each member gains an understanding of the meaning and interpretation of the team score. But it is often more convenient for the member who first completes his or her own scoring to complete the team scoring, collecting individual scores from members as they finish, and then computing the team score.

Having the learners score their own answers is an important part of this design. Self-scoring enables learners to better understand the subsequent interpretation of scores and satisfies their natural curiosity about which of their answers are correct. Self-scoring also provides a change of pace during a long session, frees the instructor from a repetitive and mechanical task, and precludes learners from complaining that their tests were incorrectly scored.

The individual scoring permits each learner to evaluate the thoroughness of his or her preparation. The team score indicates the extent to which team members were able to sort out information, facts, and data, and reach logical conclusions to arrive at a team decision. When team interaction is effective, the team score will be higher than any of the individual prework scores, an indicator of the synergy resulting from effective learning during the teamwork.

A comparison scoring chart (Figure 1) can be used to show the results of the several learning teams. For this chart, the lowest and highest scores are reported, but the names of the scorers are not. The learning efficiency score, calculated according to the formula shown in Figure 2, enables the team to compare how well it performed against how well it *could* have performed had it effectively used its resources. Thus, the important

Figure 1. Comparison Scoring Chart.

Team	A	B	C
Lowest Score			
Highest Score			
Average Individual Score			
Team Score			
Learning Efficiency Score			
Rank			

measure is not how high a team scored, but, rather, how efficiently it used its resources. The measure of team resources is
the average individual score of its members, which represents
the members' general level of preparation. This average score is
then compared to the team score. If the team score is higher
than the average individual score, the team has a gain; if the
team score is lower, the team has a loss. The average individual
score is also compared to a perfect score to determine the nu-
merical value of possible improvement. By dividing the team
gain (or loss) by the possible-improvement value, one determines the team's learning efficiency score.

A team's learning efficiency score is expressed as a positive percentage if the team posted a gain (team score higher
than the average individual score). The efficiency score is negative if team posted a loss. Figure 3 illustrates the calculation of

Figure 2. Calculating Learning Efficiency.

Record the team score. $\longrightarrow$ _____ (A)

Record the score each team member   _____ (B)
made on the test. $\longrightarrow$ _____
_____
_____
_____

Add the individual scores and record the total. $\longrightarrow$ _____ (C)

Divide the total (C) by the number of team members to
find the average individual score. $\longrightarrow$ _____ (D)

Subtract the average individual score (D) from the team
score (A) to find the gain or loss. (A gain occurs when the
team score is more than the average individual score; a
loss occurs when the team score is less than the average
individual score.) $\longrightarrow$ _____ (E)

The perfect score for this activity is: $\longrightarrow$ _____ (F)

Subtract the average individual score (D) from the perfect
score (F) to find the possible improvement. $\longrightarrow$ _____ (G)

Divide the gain or loss (E) by the possible improvement
(G) and multiply by 100 to find the team learning
efficiency score. $\longrightarrow$ _____ (H)

the learning efficiency percentages for team A, which gained 10
points, and team B, which lost 10 points.

Segment 3: Interpretation of Scores

Each team first discusses the team gain or loss. The following principles should be used to guide their interpretation of
the scores:

• A substantial loss (team score well below the average individual score) suggests that discussion was not fruitful and that
  procedural or process issues prevented the team from more
  fully using its resources. Further, if the team score is near or

Figure 3. A Comparison of Learning Efficiency After Team Discussion.

Team A: Gain

Team score = 60 (A)

Individual scores of five members (B)

40
45
50
55
60

Total team score 250 (C)

Average individual score = 50 (D)

Gain [(A) − (D)] = +10 (E)

Perfect score on test = 100 (F)

Possible improvement [(F) − (D)] = 50 (G)

$$\text{Learning efficiency} = \frac{\text{Gain (E)}}{\text{Possible improvement (G)}}$$

$$= \frac{+10}{50} \times 100 = +20\% \text{ (H)}$$

Team B: Loss

Team score = 40 (A)

Individual scores of five members (B)

40
45
50
55
60

Total team score 250 (C)

Average individual score = 50 (D)

Loss [(A) − (D)] = −10 (E)

Perfect score on test = 100 (F)

Possible improvement [(F) − (D)] = 50 (G)

$$\text{Learning efficiency} = \frac{\text{Loss (E)}}{\text{Possible improvement (G)}}$$

$$= \frac{-10}{50} \times 100 = -20\%$$

equal to the lowest individual score, the team may conclude that the most uninformed person was the most influential in the discussion.

- A small gain or loss suggests that discussion was of no help but neither was it of any harm.

- A substantial gain that nonetheless did not yield a team score as high as the highest individual score suggests that discussion was helpful but that some resources remained untapped.

- A team score that exceeds the highest individual score is one measure of synergy and indicates that members combined their partial knowledge to reach a teamwide understanding superior to any individual's understanding prior to discussion.

The discussion of the learning efficiency scoring thus enables learners to evaluate the quality of their interaction. Of course, the learning efficiency formula need not always be used. At times, recognition of the highest team score is sufficient to heighten motivation and to increase competition among teams.

As teams interpret their scores, they may also review the rationale for correct answers given in the answer key. Keys that provide an explanation of why each false answer is incorrect are particularly useful in helping learners strengthen their understanding and clarify sources of misunderstanding. The key and rationale, however, are not to be taken as absolute. Learners may be stimulated to conduct further investigations should they wish to contest the key.

If a dispute arises as to the correctness of the answer key, it should be resolved in a nonauthoritarian way, that is, by discussion and not by anyone's insistence that the key be accepted at face value. Rather, the answers and rationale are accepted as the best answers and reasoning the designer could discover.

Segment 4: Critique of Teamwork

During a critique period, team members review their performance in order to assess how well they worked together and how they might improve future individual and team performance. Learners new to the design may need forty-five minutes to an hour for the critique. As they become familiar with the critique process, only fifteen or thirty minutes may be needed. The general questions to be discussed include: Was individual learner preparation adequate? Did any one person dominate the discussion or persuade other members against their judgment to select an incorrect answer? Did members rely too heavily on compromise rather than examining the fundamental issues and achieving full agreement?

Critique instructions can be varied from time to time. For example, on one occasion critique instructions might be focused on each person's contributions to the team answer relative to his or her individual performance. Team members would then explore the following questions:

- Did any person have the correct answer to each of the questions missed by the team? Why were his or her resources not used?
- Were any questions answered correctly by the team but missed by all individuals? If so, what caused the team to reach the correct conclusion? If by something other than good luck, how could the team take advantage of this approach in the future?
- How could individuals prepare more effectively for teamwork?

Beyond contributing to future study habits and teamwork, team critiques promote social and emotional learning, enhancing learners' interpersonal skills and social competence. Although the acquisition of teamwork skills is not the primary goal of synergogic learning, such skills constitute an important secondary gain.

Segment 5: Evaluation of Individual Progress

If an alternative equivalent version of the test was created, it can be used by individuals at some later time to determine their retention of what they learned. This testing may be useful for grading purposes or for assessing each learner's degree of readiness to move on to a more complex or difficult level of subject matter.

Sample TED

The instruments presented in the following pages, adapted from materials provided by British Gas Corporation, represent excerpts from a course on writing instructional objectives taught to industrial trainers. The text on writing training objectives presented here is a portion of the prework assignment. It is followed by a brief sample of the multiple-choice questions, answer key, and rationale.

Overview of the Team Effectiveness Design for Writing Training Objectives

Learning Activity

This design is intended to develop your understanding of the theoretical basis and practical application of the pamphlet *Writing Training Objectives.*

Segment 1: Individual Preparation

In this segment you will study the pamphlet *Writing Training Objectives* and complete the accompanying multiple-choice questionnaire.

Segment 2: Teamwork

In small learning teams you will review your answers to the questionnaire. After discussion your team should try to reach agreement on the best answer for each question. At this stage, you and your team colleagues should *not* refer to the pamphlet, only to your completed copy of the questionnaire.

Time available is _____.

Segment 3: Interpretation of Scores

In a general session you will receive the answer key and the rationale for the correct answers. All participants will discuss the main issues and review their own and their team's learning.

Time available is _____.

Segment 4: Critique of Teamwork

Learning teams will critique their effectiveness by exploring with each member how he or she contributed his or her resources and how he or she might have improved that contribution. Suggestions for improvement may include (1) careful listening, (2) fuller explanations of viewpoints, (3) backing off when in doubt, (4) better awareness of time management, and (5) better awareness of the decision-making process.

[*The following is made available to learners as prework.*]

Text for

WRITING TRAINING OBJECTIVES

Prepared by:

British Gas Corporation
Training and Development Department
Personnel Division
5 Grosvenor Crescent
London SW1X 7EE

Contents

Chapter One
The Training Objective Concept

Introduction

1. Training objectives are an integral part of the logical and
    systematic methods for determining training require-
    ments. The method, called the "systems approach to
    training," is a series of steps, as illustrated in Figure A.

Figure A. Systems Approach to Training.

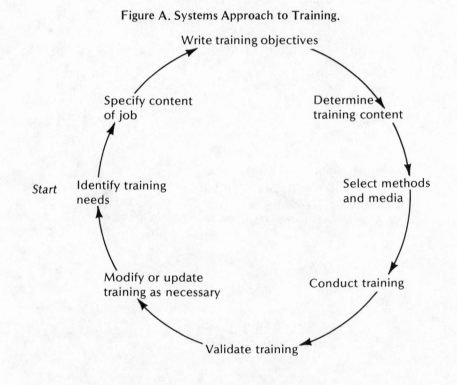

2. The design of a course of training is based ideally on a de-
    tailed analysis of the requirements of the job in terms of
    human performance. A job specification, prepared from
    the results of the analysis, describes all aspects of the job
    in considerable detail, with particular emphasis on the

range of tasks to be performed and the levels of competence required.

3.   It has been traditional to specify the training needed for a job in terms of a "syllabus," a list of subject areas to be covered in a course. Experience over many years has shown that it is much more valuable to state the training requirement in terms of behavior rather than of knowledge, specifying first what the trainee must be able to do, rather than what he must know.

4.   The concept of training objectives provides the designer of training with a method of precise specification of what the trainee must be able to do at the end of a course of training.

5.   This pamphlet is designed to provide guidance for those who are required to write or revise training objectives.

6.   The pamphlet will:
     a.   Define the term *training objective*
     b.   Distinguish different types of training objectives
     c.   Discuss the content and degree of detail required for the construction of an effective training objective
     d.   Identify the place of training objectives in the training system in relation to the identification of training needs, testing and training design
     e.   Suggest a format for sets of training objectives.
     f.   Discuss the applicability of training objectives in various areas of training
     g.   Provide examples of effective training objectives in these areas

Defining Training Objectives

Introduction

7.   Training objectives are statements that specify exactly what a trainee has to be able to do, in each separate area of his job, to demonstrate that he has reached the proficiency necessary to proceed from training to work in his particular job.

8. At the end of each stage of training the trainee should be required to perform a range of tasks, a separate training objective being set for each task. From the complete set of training objectives appropriate measures can be developed to ensure that trainees can perform according to the standards set.

Definition

9. A training objective is a description of a human performance that states:
   a. the required performance
   b. the conditions under which the performance is to be carried out
   c. the standard of performance required

Performance

10. A precise statement of what the trainee must be able to do to carry out a particular task or subtask that is part of the job for which he is being trained. Examples are:
    a. operate a dock leveler
    b. categorize payments with payment codes
    c. locate a buried main

Conditions

11. A statement of the condition under which the trainee is to perform. Examples of conditions for the preceding performances are:
    a. given a dock leveler and a vehicle to be unloaded
    b. given a list of payments: *Cashier's Manual*
    c. using approved location equipment

Standards

12. A statement of the standards of performance required, including acceptable margins of error and time limits as ap-

propriate. Examples of standards for preceding performances are:

a. checks equipment for correct working as laid down: operates controls correctly

b. correctly: as detailed in Section 8.14 of *Cashier's Manual* within 10 minutes

c. within ± 50 seconds and ± 75 mm of depth

Examples

13. Two examples of complete objectives from a set of training objectives are given in Figure B.

Figure B. Examples of Complete Objectives.

Performance	Conditions	Standards
1. Process customers' domestic gas accounts.	Showroom conditions within normal working hours. Payments tendered by cash or check. Give change if required.	Records transaction, issues receipt without error. At a rate of not less than 20 transactions per hour. Cash error rate of not more than ± 1% at end of shift. Observes security of cash as stated in section 5 of *Cashiers' Manual*.
2. Test and commission a 25 mm diameter PE Service.	From an existing 150 mm ductile iron main. Terminating at the meter control located in an external wall-mounted meter box.	Nil leakage test. Purge service to 100% gas at meter control.

The Need for Training Objectives

Introduction

14. The adoption of training objectives as the means of prescribing the training requirements leads to improvements

in training in several ways as compared with the use of the more traditional "syllabus" or list of statements.

15. A syllabus, being written in rather general terms, leaves wide scope for differing interpretation by individual instructors and examiners as to how much should be covered in instruction and in tests. This can result in skills and knowledge being taught that are not required for effective job performance, which in its turn can lead to:

   a. Unnecessarily long courses of training, with consequent ineffective use of manpower, time and other resources, within both the training function and the function from which the trainee comes.

   b. Waste of manpower, because trainees able to perform the job competently may be excluded from or perform badly on the course, through inability to cope with tasks that are irrelevant.

   c. Low job satisfaction among people who, having worked long and hard on a course, find that it is inappropriate to practice the skills and knowledge they have learned when they return to their jobs.

16. Training objectives are specific about what is to be learned and how it is intended to measure that it has been learned. If training objectives are unambiguously stated in performance terms and are then made available to instructors and trainees, everyone concerned in the learning process knows exactly what is expected. They can be a source of motivation for the trainee encouraging him to organize his thoughts and be well disposed toward the training session.

17. The use of training objectives shifts the responsibility for the content of training to a course designer, who will have access to wide sources of information as to the training requirement during the analysis of training needs. The collection of information from job holders, supervisors, managers, and experienced trainers is likely to produce a more precisely defined training requirement than relying on any one of these sources of information alone.

18. When the training requirement is expressed in the form of sets of training objectives, there then exists a firm guide

for the construction of a relevant and cost-effective training scheme. Reference to the training objectives provides a clear indication of the essential knowledge, skills, and attitudes that must be acquired during training.

Improvement in Training Efficiency

19.   For training to be efficient it must bring all trainees up to the required standards of proficiency. Trainers, however, have no sure means of deciding whether trainees have reached the required standards unless the latter can be called upon to demonstrate their newly acquired skills in such a way that they can be observed and, therefore, measured. Training objectives clearly describe what must be observed if the student is to be judged to have achieved the set standard, thus providing a yardstick against which the efficiency of training can be assessed.

Improvements in Training Effectiveness

20.   For a course of training to be effective, it should be wholly relevant to the purpose for which the students are being trained. A course can be efficient without being effective if trainees are trained to do something well that is in fact not required by the job. It is essential, therefore, that the training objectives be derived from the actual requirements of the job, ideally through an analysis of the training needs and (when appropriate) an agreed job specification.

21.   The use of training objectives as the basis of course design is essential if the effectiveness of a course of training is later to be measured through a validation study at the locations accepting former trainees. It is much more difficult to validate a course whose aims are set in the form of a conventional syllabus.

22.   Another major benefit from the use of training objectives is to be found in a greater involvement with, and commitment to, the content of centralized courses by line man-

agers. When training aims are stated in specific terms, it is possible for line managers to make meaningful comment on the appropriateness of the training for the employee's later work in the real job.

Instructions for Completing the Multiple-Choice Questions

- These questions should be answered after you have studied the pamphlet *Writing Training Objectives.*
- You may refer to the pamphlet while working through the questions.
- The questionnaire is part of a learning instrument designed to help you improve your skill in writing training objectives —it is *not* a test.
- The questions are in the conventional format of a stem and four options. In each case *one* of these options best represents the principles explained in the pamphlet and should be checked.
- Please note that several other options in each question are true, at least in part; therefore, your task is to select the *best* option for each question.
- Remember to bring both the pamphlet and the multiple-choice question paper with you to the next course meeting.

Multiple-Choice Questionnaire

1. Training objectives are statements showing
   A. the level of understanding a trainee must obtain by the end of the training.
   B. what the trainee must be able to do in order to pass from the training to the work situation.
   C. the knowledge and skill necessary to pass the qualifying test of examination.
   D. which elements of a training course are to be tested and what standard is expected.

2. The elements that constitute a training objective are
    A. statements of the knowledge, skills, and attitudes required on the job.
    B. the task to be performed, the standard of performance required, and appropriate reference to manuals or other authorities.
    C. statements that together provide a full description of the job to be done.
    D. performance statement, the conditions under which performance is required, and the standard of attainment.
3. Training objectives are a better basis for course planning than syllabuses because:
    A. Syllabuses are old-fashioned and often out-of-date by the time courses are designed to cover them.
    B. Few people can understand what the items in a syllabus actually mean whereas objectives are easily understood.
    C. Training objectives provide firm statements of what individuals are to be able to do in order to satisfy the requirements of the training identified as necessary.
    D. Syllabuses take no account of individual needs and present only a catalogue of things to be taught.
4. Efficiency in training is defined as
    A. ensuring that trainees reach the standard required by the training objectives.
    B. providing appropriate training for the objectives set.
    C. giving training only to those within the target population.
    D. confining training effort only to those areas of knowledge and skill required on the job.
5. Effectiveness in training is defined as
    A. ensuring that training is relevant to the needs of the trainees.
    B. conducting tests which ensure that training relates to the objectives.
    C. monitoring standards of training which meet the expectations of management.

D.   ensuring the relevance of both the training and test to the needs of the job and the individual.

Scoring Key and Rationale for Correct Answers

1. A. *Unsatisfactory:* Many objectives are much wider in scope than mere understanding. For most, practical performance will be required.
   B. *Key point:* Adequate performance for the job is the essential characteristic of training objectives, and the satisfactory performance of this enables the trainee to go forward into the job.
   C. *Unsatisfactory:* Objectives are specific statements of the knowledge, skill, or attitude required for a job—not simply the passing of an examination, important though this may be.
   D. *Unsatisfactory:* Training objectives are, or should be, job related such that all aspects of the job are covered. Therefore all should be tested.
2. A. *Unsatisfactory:* Training objectives can be classified as designed for the acquisition of knowledge, skills, or attitudes, but this gives no indication of what should be the essential elements of a training objective.
   B. *Unsatisfactory:* This is incomplete in that the conditions under which performance is to be carried out is a vital part of a training objective. There is not always an appropriate reference to a manual.
   C. *Unsatisfactory:* This is misleading because the job to be done is analyzed, and each element may lead to the development of one or more training objectives that may or may not be satisfied at a job performance level.
   D. *Key point:* The essential elements of a training objective are performance, conditions, and standards.
3. A. *Unsatisfactory:* This is true but training objectives can also become out-of-date unless they are revised to cover changes in practice and procedures.
   B. *Unsatisfactory:* This is also true of syllabuses, but one can go further and add that the danger lies in trainers,

examiners, trainees, and others all putting different interpretations on the items in a syllabus.

C. *Key point:* The essential strength of training objectives is that they are based on the requirements of the job.

D. *Unsatisfactory:* Taking no account of individual needs is a common failure of both syllabuses and training objectives. In the systems approach to training the needs of the individuals are taken into account when designing the training.

4. A. *Key point:* The objectives are the criteria for efficient training. If trainees attain the objectives they have been trained efficiently.

B. *Unsatisfactory:* It is the outcome of training, that is, what trainees are able to do which is important.

C. *Unsatisfactory:* Although good in principle, to train those for whom the training is designed is not the criteria for efficiency.

D. *Unsatisfactory:* If properly prepared, training objectives will all be oriented toward satisfactory job performance and training design based on them.

5. A. *Unsatisfactory:* This is only partly true; the needs of the job are of paramount importance.

B. *Unsatisfactory:* This may be a measure of efficiency but not necessarily a yardstick for measuring effectiveness.

C. *Unsatisfactory:* The needs and effectiveness of management should be taken into account at the analysis stage so that objectives take note of this.

D. *Key point:* Effectiveness has to do with ensuring that trainees can do the job for which they have been trained.

Variations on the Basic Design

There are many ways to provide richness and novelty by varying the basic design.

Prework Assignment

The basic design involves learner study of written materials. However, the prework assignment can be in the form of a movie, a play, a closed-circuit television program, tape recordings, records, still photographs, or a computer program. Let us add here that computer-assisted instruction (CAI), programmed learning, and similar innovations are broadly compatible with synergogic methods. Simply put, a computer is a delivery system that provides learners with information that they can use in any number of ways. Computers can provide directions and instructions, or questions and answers, or drills and other aids to learning.

Test Instruments

The prework test need not be a multiple-choice questionnaire. Alternative formats include questions that require ranking or locating, if a systematic basis of ordering is involved. For example, the task can be to rank cities by population, states by geographical size, countries by gross national product, companies by sales volume or profit on sales. Ranking can be an effective measure if the material has a basic order subject to objective determination and if there is enough potential uncertainty so that the teams will have initial disagreements to resolve. The design task is made even simpler by the availability of such texts as instructor manuals that include already developed multiple-choice, true-false, and other type tests.

Team Composition

Variations of team composition are possible if the design is to be used repeatedly on a series of occasions. After the first session, team composition may be changed by having teams rotate one or two individuals at each subsequent session or by creating entirely new teams.

Scoring

All scoring should be completed by the learners themselves, since scoring aids them in understanding the interpretation of the scores and learners are naturally curious to know
which of their individual answers and team answers are correct.
Learners can, however, exchange papers and score one another's answers.

Another way to vary the scoring is to increase the risk
factor by using a weighted scoring system. Weighted scoring motivates learners to think more precisely because they are penal-
ized for incorrect answers. For example, a correct answer could
receive 3 points, an incorrect answer could cost 3 points, and a
blank—reflecting students' inability to agree—could involve no
points gained or lost.

Learners can also be asked to critique their performance
and make a subjective assessment of their effectiveness prior to
scoring. This critique provides an index of the objectivity with
which they view their performance.

Strengths and Limitations

Strengths

One of the strengths of the Team Effectiveness Design is
that it, like all the synergogic designs, places the responsibility
for learning on participants themselves. As discussed in Chapters
One and Two, the design does not arouse resentments and antagonisms related to the authority-obedience model. Learners acquire knowledge directly from study materials in order to
take part in a learning experience with their colleagues. This approach might also be evaluated in the context of the democratic
process: it does advance and strengthen the concepts and skills
of active, open participation.

Another strength is the premium placed on active participation as contrasted with reactive learning. The use of multiple-
choice questions requires learners to make fine differentiations

and make explicit the subtleties of their reasoning. Participants learn to reject false or inaccurate information, facts, or data, as well as to examine why valid or correct explanations are right. To learn why something is not correct can be as valuable as to learn what is judged to be correct.

Individuals can assess their understanding by telling others their conclusions and how they arrived at them. In order for the team to be successful, members are motivated to yield on those points for which they find themselves to be unconvincing —and this in itself is important for learning. But whenever they are convinced they know the material, they are motivated to explain their answers in order to persuade others. In these ways, members learn by developing clearer convictions about their understanding or lack of it.

The team-based search for correct answers and the discussion of misunderstanding and disagreement encourage participants to strive toward complete learning effectiveness. Because all participants have studied the same material, the team is not dependent on any one person for any particular content and is not held back if one person is unprepared. Too, teams can be composed by grouping members who have a similar learning pace, which avoids the disadvantages that arise in a situation that assumes that all students learn at the same rate.

Two further strengths are that a design can be devised to cover a very specific topic and that a particular set of materials can be reused by many classes over a period of years. Thus even after the instructor who designed the materials has left an institution, his or her learning instruments can be used. Systematic updating of materials can keep them timely and pertinent to emerging knowledge.

Limitations

The use of objective questionnaires for confirming conclusions, based on answers that can be checked against the text, is not particularly suitable for subjects that place a premium on imagination, judgment, interpretation, or creativity. For such subjects, the Performance Judgment Design (Chapter Five) is more appropriate.

A second limitation is that the design depends heavily on the quality of the instruments: the manuscript, the design of the test, the validity of the key, and the comprehensiveness of the answer key's rationale. That is, the learners' educational achievements are unlikely to be better than the material they are given.

Third, team effectiveness requires some degree of interpersonal competence. If participants have inadequate interaction skills, they will need more guidelines and instructions for conducting effective discussions and critiques. Although procedural skills may limit some teams, because such skills are critical to the learners' development as effective persons, acquiring such skills should be a central focus of education.

Slow-learning students and those whose academic experiences have been frustrating to them may pose temporary problems. The spirit of sharing and of competition that the design produces motivates both kinds of students to participate, but they are likely to be disadvantaged by poor attitudes toward preparation or insufficient preparation. Such students need special help to increase their readiness for team-based participation. Some will benefit from tutoring by another student, while others may need various forms of personalized programmed instruction. These kinds of procedures can aid individuals with lower levels of mastery to catch up with colleagues in order to participate in team learning.

Applications

This design has been widely employed to address a broad variety of subjects. Examples of industrial and commercial applications include:

- Aiding supervisors and union officers in becoming more fully informed as to the content of a union contract
- Study of factory safety regulations and procedures by super-

visors and wage and hourly personnel whose jobs are hazardous

- Study of new organization structure and its intended functioning by executives, managers, and supervisors
- Study of job descriptions by entry personnel
- Study of federal regulatory requirements by plant managers
  and superintendents
- Study of corporate strategic plans by top executives of an
  aerospace company
- Study of company and competitor products by the marketing and sales personnel

The Team Effectiveness Design has been employed in the
academic setting in many subject areas—including English, psychology, sociology, fine arts, mathematics, chemistry, and physics—and in applied areas that include engineering, business administration, counseling, social work, and academic administration.

4

∞c ᒣᐤᒍᐤ ᒣᐤᒍᐤ ᐤ

Acquiring Knowledge
Through Presentations
by Team Members

The Team-Member
Teaching Design (TMTD)

∞c ᒣᐤ   Two premises direct the construction of Team-Member Teaching Designs. The first is that certain benefits accrue from a division of labor at the level of preparation, that is, each participant studies a different part of the subject matter to be learned by all. The second premise is that each learner can teach his or her team members; thus each member will serve both as teacher and student.

When learners understand that team effectiveness depends on each individual's learning a section of the material and then teaching it to the others, they are motivated to help their team by studying their assigned sections and being thoroughly prepared for the teamwork session. During that session, learners are motivated to learn, so as to contribute to the team score, and also to help the team member who is teaching to be as successful as possible. Only by helping one another in this way can a team maximize its learning.

The TMTD permits a great deal of subject matter to be covered by a study team in a short period of time. The division of preparation is particularly suitable if the educational goal is to survey a broad area rather than to study a topic in depth.

55

Overview of the Design

Segment 1: Individual preparation by learners
Segment 2: Teamwork
    Team-member teaching
    Testing
    Scoring of individual answers
Segment 3: Interpretation of scores
Segment 4: Critique of teamwork

The material to be studied is divided into equal portions, and each learner in a study team is assigned a different portion for prework study. The learner prepares a presentation to teach the others his or her assigned portion during the subsequent team session.

After team-member teaching, each learner completes a test covering all the material. Tests are scored and interpreted. During the critique session, members assess both their actual learning and the strengths and weaknesses of each member as a communicator of knowledge. This latter critique offers significant secondary benefits for increasing the personal effectiveness of managers, trainers, staff specialists, and other professionals who are called upon to exercise presentation skills.

Design Preparation

Selection of the Text

Several considerations merit attention in selecting the text to be used. The text should be divisible into as many coherent parts as there will be learners on each team, usually three to five. These parts should be approximately equal in length and roughly comparable in difficulty. A final consideration is that each of the parts must be understandable without reference to the other parts. This consideration is important because each learner studies only one part and must be able to understand that part independent of information contained in teammates' parts.

Of course, as in any assignment, the material should be of

sufficient difficulty to challenge the learners but not so difficult as to overwhelm them.

Writing the Test

The rules and guidelines for writing tests provided in Chapter Three apply here as well. The object of the test is to permit learners to measure how much they have learned from one another's presentations. The key and rationale should help them identify misunderstandings and correct them. In this design, true-false tests are often used because they sample learners' knowledge more quickly than multiple-choice or essay tests, although these can be used as well.

Creating Teams

Learners can be arranged into teams on a planned random basis, depending on learning objectives. The size of each team depends on learners' reading comprehension level, amount of technical experience, and other such relevant factors. Teams can range from two or three to seven persons. Their size is also a function of the number of parts into which the topic can be divided.

Implementing the Design

Segment 1: Individual Preparation by Learners

Each learner is assigned a portion of material for preparation. At this point, each learner receives only his or her assigned portion. This arrangement ensures that learners will truly learn the material from one another and not from reading all the portions.

Students are made aware that the measure of their learning is to be demonstrated on a test that covers all the portions of material assigned to various team members. If the team demonstrates perfect learning effectiveness, each learner will have a complete understanding of all the material.

Ground rules are established in advance as to whether

learners may use notes, an outline, or charts in their presentations, the total time available for presentation discussion, and
the like.

Segment 2: Teamwork

Team-member teaching. When a team assembles, one
learner starts by teaching the others his or her particular part of
the assignment. This team member may use whatever notes or
aids have been authorized but does not refer directly to the
original material. Other learners can ask questions, disagree,
take notes, or cross-examine—in short, they do whatever they
feel will help the learner who is teaching express the points
most completely and comprehensibly. Each member, in turn,
presents a new portion. The order in which learners teach other
members may be sequential or random, depending on the subject. If the topic is the life of Lincoln, for example, students
would present their portions in chronological order. If the topic
has parts that are nonsequential—such as the properties of five
different chemical agents—it makes no difference who teaches
first.

As an example in which individual expertise is relevant
but sequence is not, consider a technical group in a corporation
that is entrusted with making an in-depth study of a significant
competitor. Each member is responsible for presenting one aspect of the competitor's operation: financial position, manufacturing processes, marketing approaches, research and development strategy, and personnel practices. Before producing an
integrated report, team members each teach one another to
maximize their understanding of those components outside
their area of expertise. Once each can see the whole, that is, the
total picture of their competitor, the team can make a comprehensive evaluation.

The team-member teaching session concludes with learners summarizing the various conclusions from the assignment.
The instructions for this summary depend on the subject matter
but are formulated in such a way as to (1) permit comparison of
similarities and differences, (2) trace longitudinal trends, (3) gen-

eralize on a sampling basis, or (4) project implications for the future or for other points of applications and other ways of generalizing.

Testing. At this point, each person takes a test on the entire subject. Questions cover all the segments, their interrelationships, and generalizations from the material. The test contains an equal number of questions from each of the parts and several general comprehension questions relevant to the material.

Scoring of individual answers. Learners are given an answer key and rationale and score their tests. Learners' success is based on four main considerations. First, there is the thoroughness of each member's preparation, since a student can teach others only what he or she already knows; and second, each member's skill in communicating what he or she knows. Third, success depends on each person learning the information the others are able to teach. Fourth, success is related to the skill with which members listen, analyze, probe, check, and test whatever each member says, thinks, or concludes. Thus cooperation among team members is the key to success.

This design's method of measuring learning enables learners to evaluate the extent to which they know the entire subject. It also permits each team to evaluate how well it performed as a learning unit as compared with other teams.

Segment 3: Interpretation of Scores

Learners can first use their individual scores to assess how much of the subject they understand, which is an indication of individual progress in learning. An individual's score also provides a basis for measuring the additional learning needed to achieve 100 percent comprehension as measured by the test.

Next, each team can calculate its average individual score. This average indicates how well the team as a study group understands the material.

Third, learners should note their score on the part that

was their responsibility to teach. By averaging these individual scores, each team can compare the thoroughness of its members' preparation with those in other teams. Such comparison motivates better preparation on future assignments.

Fourth, a team can make a within-team comparison of how well each team member taught his or her portion. By comparing A's score on the part A taught with the average scores of B, C, D, and E on that portion, members can see how well A taught what he or she knew. The smaller the difference between the individual and average scores, the greater the teaching and learning skills generated by the team's interaction, unless, of course, a student was totally unprepared.

Segment 4: Critique of Teamwork

Using their scores as indicators of effectiveness, team members can critique several aspects of their learning.

The teamwork critique may begin by concentrating on the procedures the team members employed, such as their management of time, awareness of participation, resolution of conflicts, and discrimination between relevant and irrelevant topics. Teams can assess whether time allocations to each presenter were appropriate to the subject and whether they were adhered to. Particular attention should be placed on exploring the questions that were asked of each presenter. Did these questions aid the presenter to clarify or fill out his or her formulations? Did they lead to simple yes or no answers that did little more than eliminate a possibility without providing the rationale? Also, teams should discuss any disagreements or conflicts that arose between presenters and listeners or among listeners. Other aspects of team interaction may also be addressed.

Teams can then assess the effectiveness of each member's contribution as a teacher. Figure 4 presents an example for such an evaluation. Each individual's preparation is also discussed. Learners can discover how each person prepared and make suggestions for study methods that could have improved his or her understanding of the subject. Also subject to examination are the methods members used to prepare their presentations. Did

Figure 4. Assessment of Learners' Teaching Effectiveness.

Rate each team member from 1 = ineffective to 5 = effective on each of the items.				
Items	Team Member			
	Bill	Jill	Alice	Jose
Was he/she confident of the facts presented?				
Did he/she separate and emphasize important in contrast with less important aspects of information?				
Were points presented in a logical, orderly sequence?				
Did he/she hold convictions when challenged?				
Did he/she ask questions for clarification to ensure accuracy of understanding?				

they undertake a mental rehearsal or a mock presentation alone or to others? Were visual aids prepared in the form of outlines, pictures, charts, or figures?

Members can also coach one another as to communication strategies that would have been more effective in teaching their portions. By consulting the key, they can identify questions team members answered correctly or incorrectly. They can then determine how well the presenter communicated the key points and whether the presenter omitted key points. The rationale can thus be used as a basis for evaluating the validity of the presentation.

Another critique activity is for team members to analyze their procedure for collecting and interpreting the information each person was responsible for, and to examine how these procedures might be improved.

Because these critiques involve discussion of members' personal competencies and team contributions, team-member teaching designs require participants to be willing and able to constructively and tactfully evaluate one another. Thus these designs are most effectively used with teams whose members feel at ease in critiquing one another's performance and whose members have the interpersonal skills adequate for such activity. In general, team-member teaching designs are best used *after* other team learning designs—such as the TED, in which the critiques are less personal—have been used.

Sample TMTD

The instruments presented in the following pages represent excerpts from a course on the relationship between productivity and social forces in the work place. The text assigned for this course was *Productivity: The Human Side.* * We here present the instructions given to the learning teams, and a sample of the true-false questionnaire, answer key, and rationale.

Overview of the Team-Member Teaching Design for Studying Productivity

Task Objectives

The purposes of this activity are to:

- Develop your understanding of how social forces in the workplace impede or enhance productivity;
- Gain feedback from others as to how your own effectiveness in presenting information could be increased.

Segment 1: Individual Preparation by Learners

The study text is *Productivity: The Human Side.* All learners will read the preface and chapters 1 and 2, which provide a common orientation and background. As individual prep-

*R. R. Blake and J. S. Mouton, *Productivity: The Human Side* (New York: AMACOM, 1981).

aration, each team member will in addition study three chapters of the book. In each three-person team, member A will study chapters 3, 4, and 10; member B will study chapters 5, 6, and 11; and member C will study chapters 8, 9, and 12. Chapters 3 and 4, 5 and 6, and 8 and 9 each present different social factors influencing productivity; chapters 10, 11, and 12 give case illustrations.

Study your assigned part and be prepared to present its contents to the other members of your team during the upcoming session. At that time you will each teach your teammates your overall understanding and comprehension of your portion. You may not consult the text during your presentation, but you may use notes if you choose. When you are teaching your portion, avoid adding content that is not in the text. If you do want to add something, make it clear to the others exactly when you depart from and return to the text.

Segment 2: Teamwork

Team-member teaching. Each team should work out its rules for proceeding, for example, the order and time limits for the presentations. Include time for others to question each presenter on unclear or undeveloped points. You could decide that presenters should not be asked questions until they have finished or that members are free to interrupt during a presentation for the purpose of seeking clarification. You may wish to designate checkpoints at which you will stop to consider the quality of progress and to introduce needed improvements.

Testing. Team members' knowledge of the entire body of material will be evaluated by a true-false test. Members will individually complete the test.

Scoring of individual answers. Each team member will score his or her own test. The score of individual members will be taken as a measure of a team's teaching and learning effectiveness.

Segment 3: Interpretation of Scores

By comparing members' scores on the portions taught by each member, you will have one measure of members' teaching effectiveness. Other measures will be discussed during the critique of teamwork.

Segment 4: Critique of Teamwork

Each team member will complete the assessment form (Figure A) in preparation for discussing each team member's contribution to the learning task. As a team, discuss each member's behavior as a teacher and as a learner, and give recommendations to increase one another's effectiveness.

True-False Test

Indicate whether each of the following items is true or false according to the material presented in *Productivity: The Human Side*. In completing this questionnaire, you should not rely on your opinions but on the content of the written document. Circle *T* if the item is true, *F* if the item is false.

Chapters 3, 4, and 10

T F 1. Understanding the influence of norms on behavior is made more difficult because people tend to see their beliefs as original to themselves.

T F 2. The phenomenon of convergence occurs when people are able to reinforce one another's interpretation of objective reality.

T F 3. After convergence has occurred it continues to dictate how people react to similar experiences.

T F 4. It is most likely norms will arise readily when what is ordinarily considered physical reality becomes uncertain in people's minds.

T F 5. Once convergence has occurred the influence it has is almost invisible.

Figure A. Assessment of Team Members' Teaching and Learning Skills.

Team Members			Check which behavioral descriptions apply (I) when the person was a presenter and (II) when the person was a learner
A	B	C	
			I. Presentation Skills
			1. Ideas are presented clearly and simply.
			2. Ideas follow one another in a logical flow.
			3. Implications of concepts are drawn.
			4. Gives examples to help clarify meaning.
			5. Asks others for questions or checks to ensure that he or she is being understood.
			6. Responds defensively if questioned.
			7. Listens attentively to feedback from others.
			8. Appears relaxed, not tense.
			9. States feelings or beliefs.
			10. Tends to "make speeches."
			11. Summarizes main points.
			12. Demonstrates thoroughness of preparation.
			II. Learning Skills
			1. Listens attentively, does not interrupt speaker.
			2. Asks questions for clarification.
			3. Paraphrases points to ensure understanding of concepts or implications.
			4. Is open and direct in communication.
			5. Gets the discussion off track by pursuing irrelevant details.
			6. Blocks others' learning by defensive or hostile remarks.
			7. Tends to take over and keep the floor.
			8. Gives little indication of understanding.
			9. Checks with others to be sure they are on the same wave length.

Chapters 5, 6, and 11

T F 1. One of the unfortunate consequences of conformity in organization life is that it can create conditions which penalize innovation.

T F 2. Conformity pressures tend to keep the status quo intact even though it may be outmoded.

T F 3. If one continues to deviate from group norms his or her behavior is accepted but given little credibility.

T F 4. People are more likely to comply with the group if they have reason to believe their opinion may become known to others.

T F 5. One way to solve the problem of "lip service" is to permit people to openly express private attitudes without recrimination.

Chapters 8, 9, and 12

T F 1. The principal value of behavioral science knowledge with respect to norms is to enable managers to pattern leadership behavior according to the way others behave.

T F 2. One of the differences between a primary group and a reference group is that people are less likely to be aware of norms and standards in the primary group.

T F 3. The success of any change effort (norms shifting) requires contribution to the effort by those who lead the unit of change.

T F 4. A valuable tool for studying problems and discovering norms is the task paragraph which defines the specific issue at hand and asks for causes and solutions.

T F 5. In a norms-changing session, it is important to prevent emotions from affecting the discussion.

Scoring Key and Rationale for Correct Answers

Give yourself 2 points for each correct answer; no penalty for an incorrect answer.

Chapters 3, 4, and 10

1. T This question is true because individuals derive their attitudes, opinions, feelings, and actions from the groups

to which they belong and yet they often think of them as private and unique.

2. F   To the contrary, convergence occurs whenever there is little or no prior basis for reacting to an experience and others are experiencing the same phenomenon and expressing their reactions to it.

3. T   Although after convergence experiments people deny with increasing conviction that others had any influence on them, once convergence occurs it has a persistent influence on their reactions to similar experiences.

4. F   This question is false because norms arise more readily when circumstances are subject to interpretation than when circumstances have an objective character that can be proved.

5. T   Once convergence has occurred it feels so natural that people fail to recognize its existence. Therefore the influence it exerts is almost invisible.

Chapters 5, 6, and 11

1. T   Conformity creates the condition of people adhering to norms and clinging to attitudes that may be out of touch with the needs of the organization and even out of kilter with the times. As a result, important innovations are not made.

2. T   In the example cited the energy crisis of 1973 should have been enough to jolt the American car industry out of its prevailing "big car" norm, but it did little to shift that norm or the basic attitudes maintained within the industry.

3. F   Experiments have proved that a basic aspect of group dynamics is to enforce conformity. The price of continued deviation from a group norm is rejection.

4. T   Studies have shown that greater convergence occurs when a group member believes that his or her opinion will be made public than when it is to be kept private.

5. T   The only known antidote to the problem of "lip service" is to give those whose behavior is regulated by norms the opportunity to participate in open and candid discussions in which they can voice private attitudes.

Chapters 8, 9, and 12

1. F   Behavioral science knowledge related to norms and to
        individual attitudes anchored in existing norms is useful
        in a number of ways, but its primary value is helping to
        solve current problems.
2. F   There is no evidence to suggest that people are less like-
        ly to be influenced by the norms and standards in a pri-
        mary group as opposed to a reference group. Due to
        proximity and frequency of contact, the opposite is
        likely to be true.
3. T   There is no realistic prospect for changing norms and
        standards if those who are the leaders of the prevailing
        norm system absent themselves from the effort.
4. T   The task paragraph has two parts. The first part is an
        open, direct, and unbiased statement that identifies the
        problem. The second part asks participants what can be
        done to solve it.
5. F   In these circumstances, it is essential to create an atmo-
        sphere that allows those who are a part of the problem
        to discharge their feelings and emotions. Only in this
        way is it possible to get the negative attitudes that are
        preventing constructive problem solving out of the way.

Variations on the Basic Design

Many design variations are possible. The following examples suggest the range of learning experiences available.

Individual Preparation by Learners

To aid individuals' comprehension and communication
before they are called upon to teach, the design can include a
period during which learners meet with their counterparts on
the other teams. Thus, all members responsible for teaching portion A to their team meet as a study group to review their under-

standing of the material and discuss its presentation. These cross-team study groups can be offered a Team Effectiveness Design to guide their meetings. This is particularly useful when learners are using a TMTD for the first time because it gives them an opportunity to compare their understanding of their part with others who are studying the same part. Such comparison not only refines their understanding but also bolsters their confidence. The procedure can also be used to coach any students who have poor reading skills.

Critique of Teamwork

Cross-team meetings can also be held after the team-member teaching. Those who taught the same segment to their respective teams can review how well each performed and discuss difficulties unique to their portion of the subject matter. They can also counsel one another on improving their preparation and communication skills.

Critiques can also be directed toward specific relevant skills. For example, members could focus on proactive listening skills that promote understanding. During the critique, members could discuss the use of the following statements and questions as strategies for proactive listening:

- Tell us more about it.
- Let me say what I think is true. Is that right or wrong?
- Does that point include the following?
- I can't tell if that point was in the text or if you added it.
- Let me see if I can repeat what you said to be sure I understand it.
- Can you give me an example?
- Let me give an example and you tell us if it is a correct interpretation.

After members discuss their skills in proactive listening, they can review their experiences with other team members for critique of effectiveness.

Timing

The basic design can also be varied by administering the test on portion A immediately after that portion is presented and having the critique of that portion precede the presentation of portion B. The benefit of this variation is that each succeeding member learns how to strengthen his or her presentation from the earlier critiques. The designer's initial preparation of such a design can be time-consuming, but once the design is perfected, it can be applied repeatedly with little or no modification.

Strengths and Limitations

Strengths

The team-member teaching model is particularly useful when a broad survey of a subject is desired rather than an in-depth study. For example, if many members of a corporation need to acquire a comprehensive overview of relevant policies, a TMTD might be more useful than a TED in providing a general framework of understanding. The design would provide each person with the pertinent information without each having to consult all the corporation's procedures, manuals, guidelines, and the like.

A TMTD team of five or six learners can create an informal atmosphere that promotes spontaneity and active learning. Because each member contributes to the team's overall success by learning and communicating his or her part, this spontaneity is balanced with responsibility. As a result, the learning experience can be both fun and productive. Also, each member's responsibility to teach the others provides exceptionally strong motivation for thorough individual preparation. Since individuals can do well only by understanding the individual presentations, they are highly motivated to listen, probe, question, and clarify in a constructive manner.

A TMTD establishes a proactive learning situation that requires learners to actively participate. They cannot simply mentally rehearse their understanding while sitting silently in a classroom. The small size of the team also eases any learners' discomfort in expressing themselves. Learners are not faced with speaking to a large audience, such as a class of thirty-five, and this decreases their fear of failure or embarrassment. Furthermore, teams of three to seven members are small enough that no member can take a passive or nonparticipating role and be ignored by more active and outgoing teammates. Everyone must take part since each learner is a necessary contributor to the team's comprehension of the entire subject.

The design is also conducive to learners' developing more constructive attitudes toward preparation and participation. Most participants will want to be regarded as a good team member and to enjoy the self-respect that comes from others' recognition of good performance. A spirit of cooperation is reinforced because any individual who acts in an unconstructive way draws the disapproval of others for wasting their time.

A significant secondary learning benefit of the design is the development of platform or presentation skills by those who have not had formal speaking or presentation training. In addition to practicing their presentation skills, learners receive an objective assessment of their skills (in the form of their teammates' test scores) and a subjective critique.

For all the preceding reasons, TMTDs are of unusual value in the training of trainers and others for whom presentation and communication skills are essential, such as line or staff managers. Similarly, the design can be of inestimable value to college teaching assistants, instructors, and new assistant professors. But it has also been found useful to veteran professors who want to refine their instructional skills. In sum, the evaluation and critique of presentation skills can aid a variety of individuals and groups in gaining an increased awareness of themselves and the effectiveness of their communication skills.

Limitations

One limitation on the use of the design derives from the character of the learning material to be addressed. The design cannot be used with material that resists division into equal and independently intelligible portions.

Another limitation is that this design is most useful for students whose learning skills and achievements are roughly homogeneous. Excessive differences in learning ability render the design ineffective, though moderate individual differences can be reduced by additional coaching and preparation prior to the presentations.

Students who are competent but have developed poor attitudes toward learning may resist becoming sufficiently involved in the design to discover its advantages. This resistance to learning can sometimes be overcome by pilot testing the design and discussing any resistance with students. A careful introduction should enable alienated students to discover how rewarding learning can be.

Some learners may initially resent being evaluated not only on what they have studied but also on their presentation skills. One way to reduce or eliminate this resentment is to review with learners the criteria for evaluation well in advance of their presentations. They can then use the criteria in developing their presentations. In general, however, learners want and appreciate helpful critiques from their peers. They are especially open to advice and criticism presented in the absence of an authority figure. If no authority is present to judge learners or threaten their self-esteem, most people can readily accept feedback and critique from their colleagues.

Applications

Industrial training applications of this design are numerous. Consider a group of supervisors who need to understand a union contract in order to effectively administer it. The supervisors could assemble in five-person teams, with one member responsible for teaching a part of the contract: grievances, safety, working conditions, and so on. In a similar way the design can be used to study civil rights legislation, to investigate a record of accidents and determine hazards, or to examine a multiple-phase operation. The concepts and procedures used in a management-by-objectives program can also be segmented and learned in this manner. Because the design frees individuals from having to study the entire text, they have more time for discussion and debate of relevant issues.

The design can also be used at higher managerial levels to contribute to executives' overall knowledge of corporate operations. For example, a company's president might want all top executives to become familiar with competitor companies. The training and development department could develop a set of standard materials for each competitor, which would include the annual report, brochures or descriptions of products, the Standard & Poor ratings of the company, and so on. Each member of the executive committee would receive the materials for one competitor, and the committee would implement a TMTD. The design could include a final generalization segment in which the committee would summarize the implications of what they learned about their competitors for the manner in which they conduct their own business.

Any classroom subject that can be segmented into more or less self-contained individual parts can be learned through the TMTD approach. The design is also applicable to topics in which once all learners pool their portions they can enjoy discovering patterns, identifying common themes, and weaving generalizations. Such topics include historical and biographical subjects, industrial processes from raw materials to finished product, and comparative studies of two countries regarding their resources, climates, terrains, political systems, and the like.

Over a series of sessions, the TMTD may also be used in connection with the TED. Alternate use of the two designs provides variety and enables learners to exercise different sets of skills and responsibilities. Also, the two designs differ in the motivation they provide learners. The TMTD emphasizes thoroughness of preparation, while the TED offers the challenge and excitement of presenting one's point of view and arguing the validity of it with others.

5

৵৵৵৵৵৵৵৵

Developing Skills Through
Criterion-Based Critiques

The Performance
Judging Design (PJD)

৵৵৵৵ Central to the Performance Judging Design for the acquisition of skills is the premise that the criteria for judging skill performance need to be explicitly established and understood by the learners themselves. In traditional pedagogy, in contrast, learners usually review their instructors' assessment of their performance—for example, the grades on essays—and try to deduce the criteria from it. But the PJD enables learners to first study how to develop and apply appropriate criteria, and then to assess a performance or product executed by someone other than themselves. Learners then evaluate how other learners applied the same criteria to yet other products. Only then do learners use the evaluative criteria to judge their own performance or product. By applying effectiveness criteria to evaluate others' performances, and by becoming aware of criteria by which performance is to be judged, learners acquire a cognitive map of explicit criteria. They can then evaluate their own work and determine how to increase the effectiveness of their performance.

More specifically, the study of performances and products that reflect a variety of skill levels permits learners to make several kinds of comparisons based on the criteria of effectiveness. Learners can observe what is correct and incorrect (or effective or ineffective) in other persons' work and compare their own work with others'.

The Performance Judging Design thus avoids problems associated with both classical pedagogy and behavior modeling. In classical pedagogy, for example, teachers use their own criteria, which are often unknown to the learner, to evaluate the learner's product, as in the grading of an essay. Although the grade indicates whether the learner has done well or poorly, the criteria used in making this judgment usually have to be inferred by the learner. Without explicit knowledge of the criteria, the learner faces a trial-and-error process in which a poor grade prompts the response "Well, that's not what the teacher wanted. Next time I'll try something else."

Similar problems are associated with behavior modeling, which offers learners a model that they are to replicate in their behavior. But again, if the criteria for judging the performance are not explicit or are not comprehensive, the learner may be unsure of what constitutes an accurate replication; if the criteria are not scientifically validated, learners may be misled. Finally, when criteria are determined by someone other than the learner, it is difficult for the learner to self-critique or direct his or her own performance and to generalize from one skill area to another.

Overview of the Design

Segment 1: Individual performance by learners
Segment 2: Teamwork
  Developing criteria
  Comparing and evaluating criteria against external standards
  Groupwide agreement on criteria
Segment 3: Judging performance
  Discussion of sample performances
  Team evaluation of sample performances
  Reading critiques
Segment 4: Evaluation of progress and upgrading skills
Segment 5: Critique of teamwork

The design's objective is to help learners exercise shared responsibility for the acquisition of a skill by each member. The first segment typically involves establishing a baseline for each person's current level of skill by asking each to perform a particular task or sequence of actions. Learners then meet in teams to formulate the criteria for what constitutes an effective performance or level of skill development. These criteria are refined through comparison with external standards. Each person then applies the criteria to other persons' baseline performance, and each receives a critique of his or her own baseline performance. This performance-critique cycle is repeated until an indicated level of effectiveness is reached.

Design Preparation

External Standards

The designer provides a set of external standards that learners will use in comparing, extending, and validating the performance criteria developed by the learning teams. We term these standards *external* to indicate that they are not determined by the learners; they are, however, not external to the skill under study. For example, external standards for the performance of an electrician or plumber may include professional standards and qualifications, legislative regulations concerning practices within the industry, city codes and ordinances, and so on. A design that involves learning to write business letters may use external standards derived from any number of reference books on the subject.

To establish external standards for various technical processes, a critical-incident method may be used. Once a critical incident, whether positive or negative, has been identified because of the importance of establishing the causes that lay beneath it, it is subjected to intensive study, usually with the implication that conclusions reached can be taught to others, thus increasing or reducing the likelihood of its occurrence. The critical-incident method can be relied upon to establish criteria for safe practices, for example, because the investigation of the incident usually reveals the "causes" of the accident. By generalization, the avoidance of these causes are treated as criteria for safe practice. But the critical-incident method is not infallible, and sometimes research studies produce other explanations of the same incident.

The most reliable and valid source of external standards for many activities is scientific research. Well-designed experiments, properly replicated, provide empirically verifiable evidence for the conclusions reached.

Three main principles govern the construction of both effective external standards and team-derived performance criteria:

- The standards and criteria should be comprehensive and complete; that is, a performance should be judged in its entirety rather than according to one or another specific criteria. In this way the learner gains insight as to the entire or "whole" character of his or her performance, not just a part or segment of it.
- The standards and criteria should either have empirical validity or include a statement of their limitations.
- The standards and criteria should be understandable not only to the expert but also to the learners. No matter how rigorously formulated, if they are outside the experience of the learners or subject to multiple interpretations, they will defeat the intention of the design.

Sampling Performance

A sample must be obtained of each learner's baseline performance of the relevant skills. In a design concerned with letter writing, for example, the learners can be supplied a set of technical and factual information and asked to compose a business letter conveying this material to a designated recipient. For other designs, videotaping, role-playing enactments, trial runs, or practice presentations can be used to sample performance. If at all possible, sample performances should be recorded in some form (whether on paper or tape) for future evaluation so that learners need not rely on their memories of performances. A recording can also dramatically demonstrate to learners aspects of their performances that were "invisible" to them as they were performing.

Samples of performance can be gathered under unobtrusive or obtrusive conditions. Learners often produce a more genuine and spontaneous episode of performance when they are unaware that their performance is being observed or recorded. Unobtrusive measures are acceptable as long as the performance sample is impersonal, and the learner has the opportunity to decide whether or not the performance will be used in the design. Unobtrusive measures should never be used to bring a performance into public view against the learner's wishes.

In many situations obtrusive measures can provide a candid sample of performance, and they should be used whenever this is the case. For example, in cockpit flight-training exercises crews can simulate flight performance with cameras recording their performance. The crew members become so involved in the simulated tasks that they soon forget about the cameras.

Creating Teams

Teams may be composed with respect to considerations relevant to skill, so that no team has any advantage resulting from differences in the initial competence of members. Whether teams are homogeneous or heterogeneous, the set of sample performances or products distributed to the teams for evaluation should be as similar as possible. If the learning teams are heterogeneous, then exchange of sample performances between groups is sufficient. If teams are homogeneous, then each team should receive one product representing the most advanced group, one from the next most advanced, and so on. In this way, each team receives a sample of products from various skill levels for comparison.

The number of teams and members can vary, depending on the task, time available, and number of participants.

Implementing the Design

Segment 1: Individual Performance by Learners

Learners working individually complete a set task that demonstrates their current level of skill. For a design on writing reports, the task might be to write a two-page report on a given subject. In a corporate training design, junior executives could be provided with items of basic information on products and services and asked to prepare a transmittal letter to a prospective customer.

Segment 2: Teamwork

Developing criteria. Teams meet to develop the relevant criteria for judging effectiveness in performing the particular skill. In this discussion they will seek to make their intuitive understanding of the criteria as clear, complete, and explicit as possible. For example in a design on writing reports, each team would develop criteria for the report a highly skilled person would be expected to produce. They would be given the following written instructions: The report you are to prepare is to be sent to Mr. X for his review and approval and decisions as to whether you are to be offered a promotion [or employment or university admission]. Therefore, it is important that you prepare the report in such a way as to make it an effective presentation. The first step is to think through the explicit criteria that are likely to be used to evaluate the effectiveness of your report.

Comparing and evaluating criteria against external standards. Teams are provided with external standards, which they study and discuss to improve their understanding of what constitute sound criteria. Teams study these standards and use them to modify or expand the criteria they themselves developed. Having discussed their own standards, they are committed to them and add or replace from the external source only when their understanding and conviction so indicate. The report-writing teams could be given the following external standards:

Mr. X is considering the following criteria for evaluating a technical report:

1. The purpose of the report is clear.
2. Each paragraph treats only one major category of information.
3. All the necessary facts and information are included.
4. Data are presented in a logical, sequential order.
5. The report is concise and free of redundancy.
6. The conclusion drawn follows from the evidence provided.
7. Spelling, punctuation, and grammatical usage are correct.

Groupwide agreement on criteria. The different teams are likely to have developed different criteria. Teams now need to select the best criteria to be used for judging performances. This selection may be done by the group at large through discussion and agreement. If the group's size makes this impractical, decisions can be made in the following way: Each team receives a list of all the teams' criteria. They compare and evaluate the criteria on a four-point scale:

1 = Agree with the statement.
2 = Agree with the statement changed as follows.
3 = Need further clarifications as to what the statement means.
4 = Disagree with the statement for the following reasons.

The separate teams apply this four-point system to all the lists. In a general session differences are worked through until a single list of criteria is achieved.

Segment 3: Judging Performance

Each team is given a set of sample performances or products, and each team member is responsible for one sample. If possible, the samples should be anonymous.

Discussion of sample performances. One team member presents the sample assigned to him or her while the other members observe or listen and make notes. The team then discusses how the sample compares to the established criteria for effectiveness. They proceed to discuss each of the samples and may then briefly review each to make sure that the criteria have been applied uniformly to all samples.

Team evaluation of sample performances. The team is now prepared to identify similarities and differences between all the samples and to evaluate the strengths and weaknesses of each relative to the criteria. This evaluation should be in specific and concrete terms that will help the performer understand his sample's strengths and weaknesses. The team's conclusions are summarized in writing for each sample by the person who earlier presented it to the team. This written critique is intended to express the consensus of the team.

Reading critiques. While learners are still assembled in their teams, each is returned his performance sample with the critique. Each member presents his or her sample to the team, followed by a reading of the critique. Thus team members are able to share their own samples and their responses to the critiques. Members can help one another interpret the critiques, as well as offering additional suggestions to strengthen effectiveness.

Typical instructions to team members for this step include the following: After a member reads a critique aloud, other team members should help him or her understand the critique—both its value and its limitations—and how to use the critique to improve future performance. Discuss the following questions:

- Is the critique on target? complete? fair?
- Does the performance appear to be representative of the learner's skills?
- Do any points in the critique appear to be contradicted by the evidence presented?

- Are there additional suggestions that might aid the learner in creating a better product in the future?
- Does the team's knowledge of the learner suggest that any significant elements were neglected in the written critique?

Team discussion of such questions can often enrich the understanding and learning members gain from a critique and evaluation of their performance.

Segment 4: Evaluation of Progress and Upgrading Skills

A second performance assignment—different yet comparable, though usually of somewhat greater difficulty—is given to learners for individual work. Students use both the performance criteria previously developed and the critique of their first sample in completing this new assignment.

These performances are now judged by the teams, using the steps described in segment 3 preceding. In addition, after the new critique is discussed, teams may compare it with the learner's previous one.

This cycle of introducing additional assignments with assessment can be repeated until learners attain the desired level of skill in their performances or products.

Segment 5: Critique of Teamwork

When all performance-critique cycles are completed, teams meet to discuss the effectiveness with which they operated. The form of this critique follows that used to assess teamwork in segment 4 of the TED or the TMTD; see Chapters Three and Four, respectively.

Summary

Six learning elements are essential for skill development in the PJD:

- Before considering criteria each learner creates a sample of his or her skill.

- Each learner participates in team discussions of appropriate criteria.
- Teams contrast their criteria with established standards and produce a refined set of criteria.
- Each team evaluates the samples created by colleagues on other teams and composes a critique.
- Each member receives a critique of his or her sample and discusses both the sample and the critique with team members.
- Each person has the opportunity to apply what he or she has learned on a second assignment.

Sample PJD

The following illustration is based on a course on writing training objectives taught to industrial trainers by the British Gas Corporation. In that course, learners first complete the TED presented as a sample in Chapter Three. They then use their new knowledge to develop their skills in writing the objectives.

Following the overview of the design, we present a sample of the external standards prepared by the designer and used by learners to refine their set of performance criteria.

Overview of the Performance Judging Design for Writing Training Objectives

Learning Activities

The purpose of this design is to:

- study and perfect criteria for the effective writing of training objectives
- test the utility of criteria in assessing objectives
- practice writing training objectives
- receive colleague feedback on practice assignments

Segment 1: Individual Performance by Learners

Step 1. Assemble the materials you will use as the basis for writing training objectives. These may include any or all of the following:

- analysis of training needs (for which objectives are needed)
- existing trainer objectives (which require revision)
- incomplete training objectives (which require completion)

Step 2. Using these materials, write *at least two complete objectives.* These should be marked with your team number/ letter/color (for identification), *not* your name. Please attach the document(s) on which the objectives are based.

Available time is _____.

Segment 2: Teamwork

In your learning team and using the pamphlet *Writing Training Objectives,* develop specific examples for applying criteria for effective objective writing under the following headings: performance statements; conditions; and standards.

Teams list their criteria on a flip chart for presentation to the general session.

Available time is _____.

Segment 3: General Session

In the general session each team presents its criteria. With the help of the learning administrator, agreements between teams are identified; differences in team lists are highlighted and discussed; team lists are compared with external criteria; and a consolidated list is agreed upon for the whole course.

Segment 4: Teamwork

Individuals' written training objectives (collected at segment 1, step 2) are exchanged across teams so that one team receives the work of another team for assessment. To produce a useful critique on the work of colleagues in another team it is recommended that:

- Each member take personal responsibility for assessing the work of one member of the other team.
- After studying the work, the team draft a short assessment

statement (based on the criteria agreed upon at segment 3) and brief recommendations for improvement.

- The statements be discussed by the team and amended as necessary until agreement is reached.

The assessments and the objectives to which they relate are then returned to the authors by the learning administrator.

Segment 5: Teamwork

Assessments are reviewed by authors with the assistance of team members to critique and interpret the meaning of colleague feedback received from the other team.

Expert Criteria for Writing Training Objectives

[The following list is the set of external criteria given to learning teams in segment 3].

Performance Statements

Performance statements must:

include an *action* word indicating what is to be *done*
specify the result, product, or output rather than the method
specify an observable and measurable activity
be as precise as possible

Conditions

Any or all of the following specifications may be appropriate:

equipment, materials, aids to be used
information to be provided
location or environment in which performance is to be carried out
methods to be employed

Standards

Any or all of the following standards may be appropriate:

accuracy
sequence
time
quality
method of assessing or measuring result

Variations on the Basic Design

Team Composition

The membership of teams can be maintained over a series of learning applications, or it can be varied from one application to the next.

Development of Criteria

After teams have developed criteria, new teams are composed with each new team having one member from each of the original teams. This step permits each learner to gain a firsthand interpretation of what each team's criteria mean. In these meetings, each member reads the criteria developed by his or her own team, and members evaluate the strengths and weaknesses of each of the sets of criteria. When the original teams reconvene, they consider these recommendations and establish a final set of criteria. If markedly different criteria or interpretations have arisen, a general session may be called to achieve overall agreement and full understanding of the criteria.

In another variation of the design, criteria development can be the initial step, that is, it can precede the learners' completion of the sample performance.

A third variation calls for teams to assign grades or points to the performances they have evaluated. In this case, teams can compete on the basis of the total team scores.

Teams can also be asked to rank criteria from most to least important to an effective performance. This ranking provides a basis for emphasis, aiding learners to know which aspects deserve the most attention and effort. Learners are provided with an excerpt of a performance by a recognized expert against which they can test their rankings.

Critique of Products

The basic design described in this chapter calls for a written critique. In some circumstances, however, an oral critique may be presented directly to the person whose skill is being evaluated. If the atmosphere is supportive and learners are motivated to increase their effectiveness, critique is welcome. Furthermore, the use of agreed-upon criteria for assessments greatly heightens the objectivity of evaluations. Finally, the learning administrator may introduce the discussion topic of standards for giving and receiving feedback as a basis for learners' exploring their feelings and reactions to performance assessment.

Strengths and Limitations

Strengths

The PJD is a very effective tool for skill development. One source of its power is that students learn to use criteria for perfecting their performance of a skill. In this, the design differs from conventional approaches that treat the acquisition of a skill as a matter of mechanical repetition divorced from conceptual models. The PJD is based instead on the premise that there are objective criteria for performance; that learners must understand these criteria and their rationale; and that learners can, once they understand these criteria, constructively apply them to their own work and their colleagues' work.

A second source of the design's effectiveness comes from the premise that certain skills are requisite to the use of knowledge. This more or less self-evident truth is seen in chemistry courses, in which laboratory experience helps students better understand theoretical knowledge. But the relationship between knowledge and skills is largely ignored in many areas. For example, many business schools teach the practice of management as a series of concepts to be learned, without provision for students to acquire skills in implementing them. But when performance is viewed as a necessary complement to knowledge, when students acquire knowledge and then the skills to use it—then education has more utility. Furthermore, when students learn the general criteria in terms of which specific techniques or skills are performed, they can readily adapt their skills to changing circumstances and extend their abilities without formal instruction.

This concept of competence resulting from the acquisition of knowledge and skill defines a second type of educational synergy. When knowledge is accompanied by skill in applying that knowledge (or vice versa), the resulting competence is greater than that which can be expected from learning either alone.

Another strength of the design is that it provides many opportunities for comparison. Each learner sees how several others performed on the same activity. This arrangement is likely to induce more rapid learning than occurs when students do not see others' work. For example, when students see the errors others make, they are better able to avoid making the same errors in their own performance. The evaluation and evaluative feedback on every performance also provides a reservoir of comparisons that facilitate learning. The design thus encourages learners to develop insight based on summary and generalization, not only about their own performance but also about the overall characteristics of effective and ineffective performance.

Like the other synergogic designs, the PJD relies on teamwork rather than the pedagoic authority model. Whereas an instructor's grades may provoke a student's loss of self-esteem or hostility, critiques from colleagues usually do not. Furthermore, each learner's performance is judged against explicit criteria— thus reducing the likelihood of arguments that one's product has been subjectively evaluated or treated unfairly. Indeed, if samples are evaluated anonymously, then the critique cannot be interpreted as colored by personal feelings toward the learner and is therefore more likely to be viewed as formulated without bias. These circumstances support a motivation to improve one's performance and to be open to others' suggestions for doing so.

In addition to improving their performance, students learn to exercise evaluative judgments through critiques intended to aid others in recognizing their strengths and weaknesses. This practice contributes to each learner's ability to self-critique his or her own performance by using the same standards of judgment.

Finally, like the other synergogic designs, the PJD places the responsibility for learning on the learners and casts them in cooperative relationships to improve their effectiveness.

Limitations

The design may be inappropriate for some groups if anonymity in the samples is not possible. Even though the evaluation is objective, some learners will feel threatened by colleague critique. If learners are extremely uncomfortable with giving and receiving critiques, the design will be ineffective.

A second limitation concerns the learners' rates of progress. Difficulties may arise if one student progresses at a rate other than that of team colleagues. However, team membership can be arranged so that learners with comparable degrees of skills are placed together, allowing the best students to move at a faster rate. Similarly, whole teams of slower learners can move together to higher levels of skill, while retaining the advantages of collegial critique from other teams.

If the class or course time is limited, the amount of time needed for teams to develop criteria may pose scheduling problems. But the time spent in developing criteria is extremely valuable because of the importance of the learners' comprehending the criteria that guide the acquisition of the skill.

Applications

The design can be applied directly to the learning of any skill for which effectiveness criteria can be formulated. The sample performances may be written or recorded by audio cassette, videotape, or photographs. Other types of samples include the learner's use of a machine, such as a calculator, a computer, a typewriter, and the like. Performance that is sampled from real-life settings can also be used. For example, sales personnel can tape record an actual sale or have colleagues observe an interaction with a customer. Students in driver education courses can make notes while one student drives.

Industrial applications of the design include the training of personnel interviewers and performance appraisal training. Once teams develop criteria for what constitutes an effective interview, simulated interviews are held. A quantitative measure can be derived to assess how well the interviewer met the criteria. Since one criterion is gathering facts, the interviewee can be provided with a career history laced with absenteeism, firings, and so on. The interviewee is instructed to reveal these facts if the interviewer asks, but not to volunteer them. After the interview, both interviewer and interviewee take a test that measures what was revealed and critique the interviewer's inquiry skills. Other criteria relevant to effective interviewing are treated in a similar manner. (Uses of this design have revealed that many employment interviews lead to decisions that are based on a paucity of facts. Also, interviewers with extensive experience in selection sometimes discover that their quantitative scores prove them to be less proficient in developing facts than they had assumed themselves to be. The resulting discrepancy leads to a new interest in gaining a more thorough understanding of the interviewee.)

In applying the design, one should recognize that the character of feedback and critique depends on the nature of the performance and the dimensions that characterize that performance:

- The more spontaneous the performance (that is, the more natural), the more meaningful the feedback to the learner and probably the more valuable to him or her as a learning device.
- The more significant to the person's sense of effectiveness,

the greater the implication of the feedback; thus the critique may need to proceed in small steps to ensure that each point is clearly understood by the learner.

- The sooner the sample or simulated performance is followed by a real-life performance, the more meaningful the feedback and critique to the learner.
- The learner's receptivity to a critique will increase as the critique becomes more specific, operational, and concrete. Critiques should offer a range of evidence that enables the learner to be objectively accurate in interpreting it.
- The more descriptive and the less evaluative the feedback, the more likely it will be accepted and used by the learner.

This design can also be applied to creativity practice and imagination training. In these applications learners are first asked to develop criteria that distinguish a creative effort from an uncreative production. When these criteria have been agreed upon, learners apply them in whatever ways appropriate to preparing a creative product. The subsequent steps follow the basic design.

The PJD can also be used for solving problems in situations where expert criteria have never been developed, such as team building and interface problem solving. These applications involve issues beyond those that can be dealt with here (see Blake and Mouton, forthcoming).

6

Examining Attitudes
Underlying Effective Behavior

The Clarifying
Attitudes Design (CAD)

ᨀᢙ   Attitudes are significant contributors to or detrac-
tors from effective performance. There is little a manager can
do to motivate a subordinate whose attitudes have turned sour,
while a person who has positive attitudes toward accomplish-
ment is unlikely to be stopped even when confronted with barriers that make achievement difficult.

Attitudes are a frame of mind, a mental outlook in terms
of which a person views an activity or experience. Everyone, for
example, has an attitude toward work and judges others as hard-
working or lazy in terms of it. Everyone has attitudes toward
quality—How good is good enough?—honesty, personal reliabil-
ity, and so on. For our purposes, attitudes also encompass beliefs and values, because these too determine a person's outlook
and can be addressed by the clarification design.

Attitudes themselves are invisible, but their traces are revealed through a person's behavior on a series of occasions. The
elusiveness of attitudes, however, has led some educational theorists, such as B. F. Skinner, to reject the very notion that attitudes exist in any real way. These theorists concentrate their
attention on how people learn and acquire new behavior. Many
organizational managers adopt this position, focusing on the ra-
tional or logical areas of behavior.

Other educational theorists acknowledge the potency of attitudes but consider them a private matter. They hold that people's attitudes, in particular those concerning issues such as religion or politics, are to be accepted at face value and to be respected as personal choices. Furthermore, some argue, there are no ultimate criteria for judging private attitudes as being sound or unsound, good or bad, right or wrong, and therefore attitudes lie outside the scope of education. From this position, for an educator to propose the evaluative study of attitudes amounts to promoting private beliefs or disseminating propaganda, not education for maturity.

From a practical point of view, however, it is evident that attitudes can either impede or promote performance and that people tend to congregate with those who share the same attitudes. This social cohesion reinforces the retention of those shared attitudes, as each person knows that others feel the same way.

Although some attitudes reflect issues inappropriate perhaps for public discussion, many others are in the public domain and therefore are legitimate educational topics. Take safety or stealing as an example. Who could protest against promoting a sound attitude toward safety or a more vigilant attitude against stealing? Thus we see that we can begin to distinguish private, personal, and privileged attitudes from attitudes that have a public character. Educational intervention in the latter can enable people to become healthier, stronger, or happier, with sound attitudes as a basis for developing their lives. The model of learning described in this chapter is intended to aid learners to change attitudes that are of the public character and to bring about increased congruence between such attitudes and their expression in behavior.

The relationship between attitudes and behavior is complex. Under normal conditions, the two can be expected to be congruent. But such factors as organizational pressures, deception, Machiavellian tactics, and so on may lead people to actions that contradict their attitudes or values. Too, in some cases people do not know their own attitudes because they have not carefully articulated them. They may be unaware of how their professed attitudes contradict their actual conduct. Also, they may be unaware of attitudes alternative to their own, which they might embrace or reject once they recognize the possibilities.

The CAD aids learners to identify their own actual attitudes and to consider whether there might be sounder attitudes to guide their behavior. Thereafter each person is asked to think through how his or her behavior would be different were it to be consistent with sounder attitudes. The objective here is to bring about a congruence between desirable attitudes and behavior.

An example will clarify some of the implications of attitude change. Consider a group of ministers, all of whom belong to the same church. Each is responsible for counseling young people whose attitudes often differ from those held by many ministers. As a result, young people seeking premarital counseling go from one minister to another until they find one whose attitudes are congruent with their own. This creates conflict among the ministers, who have no shared explicit strategy for premarital counseling based on an agreement of what constitutes sound attitudes in this area. They need to compare their attitudes and study areas of inconsistency or contradiction. Such discussion is difficult, however, because few ministers want to face the criticism of colleagues for being too liberal or too conservative in premarital counseling. The clarification design described in this chapter would allow them a format in which such discussion would be possible and effective.

While the preceding example is concerned with counseling across a generation gap, many other attitudes are equally subject to clarification. In the workplace these include attitudes toward the union, safety, quality, productivity, and an endless number of other concerns that influence workers' effectiveness as well as satisfaction.

In summary, this design is useful in helping individuals to (1) become more aware of their present attitudes, (2) appreciate a spectrum of alternative attitudes, and (3) make a deliberate choice regarding attitudes that are soundest in a given set of circumstances.

Overview of the Design

Segment 1: Individual preparation by learners
Self-assessment
Ranking a range of alternatives
Segment 2: Teamwork
Ranking of attitude alternatives for soundest
Examining differences between soundest and actual
Planning for personal behavior change
Segment 3: Developing a shared norm of conduct
Segment 4: Individual reranking of attitudes
Segment 5: Critique of attitude changes
Segment 6: Critique of teamwork

The design preparation for this design includes the selection of the attitudes for study and the writing of an attitude questionnaire, usually a multiple-choice inventory. Each learner independently completes the questionnaire by selecting from the range of given alternatives the ones that most accurately represent his or her views. Next, teams meet to discuss and reach agreement on which of the attitude alternatives represents the basis of soundest action in a particular circumstance. A comparison of the consensus and the actual attitudes of each member provides a basis for each person to develop a plan for changing his or her behavior so it will be more consistent with the team's agreed-on choice of a soundest attitude. In a general session, each team presents its consensus, and the entire group works to develop an agreement on norms that will influence their behavior. Thereafter each person, working alone, reranks the original attitude alternatives to represent his or her current thinking. These rerankings are the subject of a personal or team critique of attitude change. A critique of the team's process skills completes the activity.

Design Preparation

The most significant aspect of the design concerns selecting the attitude for study and writing the questionnaire alterna-

tives, which will constitute the range of possibilities that learners consider in assessing their personal positions and developing
the soundest basis of action.

Selecting Attitudes for Study

Attitudes for study should be relevant to the educational
issues in a class or central to effective performance in school or
on the job. For example, gaining agreement among supervisors
about the desirability of a subordinate's participation in setting
objectives is central to the implementation of a management-by-
objectives program.

Second, the design is likely to be most effective if the
attitudes chosen for study are those likely to arouse disagreement and contention. Topics that do not elicit a wide range of
intense attitudes are not likely to produce useful discussions.
Further, if most learners' behavior is already consistent with
sound attitudes on a given topic, discussion can add little.

Writing an Attitude Questionnaire

Identify in operational terms the attitude to be measured.
For example, any of the following might be the basis for a design: getting to work on time, double-checking typing for perfect accuracy, controlling office expenses, or feelings toward
the company.

Consider the range of possible attitudes toward the given
subject: strongly negative, neutral, strongly positive. Prepare as
many statements as necessary to express the full range (rarely
fewer than five or more than seven). For example, consider this
range of employees' attitudes toward their company:

- "I hate the company. It's a lousy place to work" (poor pay,
  bad hours, unfair supervisors, oppressive working conditions,
  sour colleagues).
- "I'd rather work for another company, but this job is good
  enough until something better comes along."
- "It's okay. Not the best but not the worst either. It's an
  easygoing, live-and-let-live kind of place."

- It's a good place. Interesting people and work, reasonable pay, good benefits."
- "I love it. It's challenging and rewarding. I want to help make the company better."

As a pilot or "test" sample, ask a few people to rank the alternatives from the ones they most strongly endorse to the ones they least agree with. Ask them to briefly explain why they ranked the alternatives as they did. Ask questions to improve your understanding of their choices. This pilot test should provide you with a range of attitudes, some of which are likely to be different from your own. This diversity should be reflected in the construction of the final scale. The pilot test will also help you identify alternatives that appear ambiguous or unclear.

Again for pilot purposes, ask other people to rank the alternatives from the *soundest* attitude to the worst attitude a person could have. If everyone picks the same alternative, the item may not be a useful one since there will be no basis for discussion of soundest alternatives. However, if everyone in this sample feels the same about what is soundest and yet most people in the earlier sample did not choose that alternative as descriptive of their actual attitude, the item may produce a productive discussion about the discrepancy between actual and soundest alternatives.

Creating Teams

Teams are usually composed on a planned random basis. It is important that a wide range of attitudes are represented on each team. For if team members share the same attitudes, they are unlikely to challenge one another's convictions or discuss the possible value of each alternative attitude on the questionnaire. Also, if all members agree, they are likely to believe they have chosen correctly. If the majority agree on a position, colleague pressures can influence the minority, particularly a minority of one or two members, to pay lip-service agreement to the others while withholding their real convictions. Thus, diversity among team members' attitudes is needed to promote vigorous discussion, thoughtful examination of alternatives, and a meaningful consensus process. To ensure diversity, the learning administrator can preassess individual attitudes and then arrange team membership accordingly. The preassessment would involve having participants rank one set of alternative attitude statements. The learning administrator would collect these rankings and sort the individual rankings into three general categories, for example: strongly positive, neutral, and strongly negative responses. The learning administrator would then randomly assign a member from each category to the same team. If the teams are to have more than three members, the same principle can be applied to produce diversity.

Implementing the Design

Segment 1: Individual Preparation by Learners

Self-assessment. Working alone, each learner composes a statement that describes his or her attitude toward the selected topic. For example, the learning instrument might provide this instruction:

> Various attitudes are held by different people toward aspects of performance appraisal. Write a brief description of your present attitude toward each item. Answers should be at least a sentence in length and should represent your real feelings about the issue. The two items are: (1) the contribution of performance appraisal to the company; and (2) the contribution of performance appraisal to the employee.

Ranking a range of alternatives. A multiple-alternative attitude questionnaire on the selected items is then distributed to each participant. The alternatives represent the fullest possible range of attitudes toward the topic being studied. These ranges may be positive-negative, good-bad, sound-unsound, and the like, depending on the attitude under study.

Each participant is asked to read all the alternatives and to rank them. If five alternatives are given, each participant is to place a *5* next to the alternative he or she most strongly endorses as characteristic of his or her own attitude. The remaining alternatives are to be numbered in descending order of endorsement; thus a *1* will represent the alternative he or she most strongly rejects.

Each participant then examines the handwritten attitude statement previously composed to see which of the attitude alternatives is closest to his or her spontaneous expression of attitude before examining the alternatives. The letter identifying this alternative is to be placed beside the handwritten statement.

For example:

> *Instructions:* Place a *5* by the choice that best represents an expression of your personal attitudes, numbering the others according to your order of choice, to *1,* which is least representative of your attitudes.

The contribution of performance appraisal to the company:

A. If managers are doing their job, they are constantly assessing the performance of their subordinates; therefore there is little need for a formal performance appraisal system.
B. An appraisal system benefits the corporation by letting employees know that managers are interested in them; therefore relationships between manager and employee are improved.
C. An effective appraisal system maintains standards of behavior that support corporate well-being.
D. Managers and employees are best left alone to do their work as they see best; therefore a performance appraisal system is of little value.
E. A valid appraisal system can improve corporate results by motivating managers and employees to achieve high performance standards.

Now examine the statement you wrote to describe your attitude concerning the contribution of performance appraisal to the company. Place beside your written statement the letter (A, B, C, D, or E) that represents the attitude alternative which most closely resembles your statement.

Segment 2: Teamwork

Ranking of attitude alternatives for soundest. Teams then meet to rank the same attitude alternatives, but this time the criterion for ranking is the overall soundness or validity of the choices. The same ranking scale (from 5 to 1) is used, and the team strives to reach an agreed-on ranking. Members are thus encouraged to express their rationale for ranking, to question others' reasoning, and to try to persuade others to agree.

Sample instructions for this segment are:

Discuss each of the alternatives to the item and decide as a team whether it represents a truly sound position for the corporation. Avoid using a simple majority to reach your decision by talking through each alternative until everyone, if possible, agrees on the team answer. Record your team conclusions next to your individual ranking of each item. One person should have responsibility for reporting the team's conclusions in the next general session.

In the course of such discussions, many participants realize that they cannot trace the origins and development of their attitudes nor marshal evidence or logic in defense of them. Team members may come to realize that many of their attitudes, though strongly held, merely reflect what they have heard others say. This realization can be of crucial importance —if a member discovers that he or she has an unconstructive attitude and cannot explain a rationale for it, he or she may willingly decide to change that attitude to one that is more constructive and defensible.

Examining differences between soundest and actual. Once team members have agreed on the soundest statement, they examine the differences between actual attitudes and the soundest one. Although members usually have a sense of the range of convictions expressed by others, it is often useful at this time to review each person's handwritten statements or the rankings done as prework.

Planning for personal behavior change. Team members are now ready to discuss how each wants to change his or her behavior to be consistent with the agreed-on description of soundest attitudes. If appropriate, individuals may commit themselves to making specific changes in their personal behavior. Teamwork at this stage can provide significant motivation to change as well as promote commitment to the new attitude.

For the example on the value of performance appraisal, the following kinds of planning questions may be usefully asked: What are the performance appraisal problems you as a supervisor have experienced? What barriers or pitfalls do you see in making your behavior consistent with what you now regard to be the soundest attitudes? What specific steps can you take to exercise your responsibility for valid performance appraisal?

Segment 3: Developing a Shared Norm of Conduct

When all teams have completed their rankings and personal planning, a representative from each team reports the team rankings to the entire group. The learning administrator records the rankings on a flip chart to test for similarities and differences between them. Should there be significant differences in rankings, it may be desirable to spend additional time discussing the rationale for each team's conclusions.

If differences persist and a greater congruence in attitudes is important, discussions could be held with new teams, which may be constituted by rotating one or two members from each of the original teams. These new teams would examine the rationale for the earlier teams' conclusions. In this way, it may be possible to reconcile differences and arrive at a single shared norm.

Segment 4: Individual Reranking of Attitudes

Team members then each rerank the set of attitude alternatives to reflect their present attitudes toward the topic. (The reranking should be done without reference to the first ranking.) Each member then compares these rerankings with the ones completed earlier as prework.

Segment 5: Critique of Attitude Changes

The critique of attitude changes is an optional segment in the design. It may be omitted if members of the study teams are from different organizations or different parts of the same organization, or if the organization's climate or culture is marked by a high degree of distrust.

Teams explore how each participant's rankings and attitudes have changed as a result of the discussion, and if these changes have any implications for that person's behavior. This review and critique of individual attitude change and commitment to changes in behavior is of particular significance when the team members belong to the same work group. Then each person can receive help and support from others in implementing the planned changes.

Segment 6: Critique of Teamwork

The critique of the team's process follows the same pattern as that outlined for the other designs (see Chapters Three, Four, and Five). Instructions particularly useful for the CAD direct teams' attention to how attitudes and convictions were expressed and differences resolved. For example, each member could be asked to rank the following items from 5, most typical of team discussion, to 1, least typical of team discussion, during that part of the design concerned with reaching a team consensus.

Our discussion was:

A.   Flat and lifeless, dull and uninvolved; whatever ideas and opinions were expressed were said with little or no conviction.
B.   Easygoing and pleasant; polite give-and-take resulted in a harmonious session.
C.   Civil and reasonable; different opinions and ideas were expressed, and reasonably acceptable positions were reached; we adjusted our positions so as to be agreeable.
D.   Win-lose competitiveness, critical, and tense; one or more of us steadfastly held to our opinions and seemed out to prove the others wrong.
E.   Penetrating, rewarding, and challenging; ideas and convictions were expressed with candor; differences were thrashed through to sound understanding.

By discussing each member's rankings, team members can determine how much agreement exists as to the quality of their teamwork. If rankings disagree, the team should investigate the reasons for the differing opinions. The final step is for team members to examine how they can improve their process skills.

Sample CAD

The following illustration of a Clarifying Attitudes Design concerns attitudes toward responsibility for learning. The excerpt presented here includes one multiple-choice attitude scale and the instructions for prework and team discussion.

CAD for Attitudes Toward Learning

Task Objectives

The purposes of this exercise are to: (1) determine the degree of agreement within the training community regarding what are the soundest attitudes toward learning; and (2) clarify individuals' attitudes as to the fundamental issues of strategies of education.

Segment 1: Individual Preparation by Learners

A variety of attitudes are held by people toward the topics listed below. In the space provided, write brief descriptions of your *present* attitude toward each topic. The answer you give should be at least a sentence in length and should represent your real feelings about the topic.

1. Responsibility and roles of instructors and students for learning

[List of topics continues.]

Next, for the following questionnaire items, place a *6* in the left-hand column next to the choice that best represents an expression of your personal attitudes. Number the others according to your order of choice, with *1* being the statement least like your own attitude.
Available time is _____.

1. Responsibility for learning:
    A. The responsibility for learning comes from the students themselves. They should be responsible for what they learn as well as how they learn it.
    B. Through the use of participative learning designs that can be evaluated against external criteria, students can take responsibility for their own learning. The instructor's primary role is to guide them through the designs.
    C. The instructor knows more about the subject matter and environment for learning than students do and should present the subject in the most efficient manner and assume responsibility for ensuring student performance.
    D. The instructor feels an overriding responsibility and

uses reward and punishment to increase students' responsiveness to learning.

E.   Students should be responsible for identifying what they want to study and setting their own pace. The teacher can help by giving support and encouragement.

F.   Responsibility should be shared between the students and the instructor. The instructor is responsible for setting a pace the student can easily adjust to and the students are responsible for participating.

Segment 2: Teamwork

Step 1: Ranking of attitude alternatives for soundest. As a team, you are to reach agreement on the soundest ranking for question 1. *Soundest* here refers to "most conducive to promoting student learning."

Begin by having one team member read his or her ranking and explain the reasons for that ranking to the rest of the team. Then have another member do the same, and so on. Examine and question one another's rankings and reasoning in order to arrive at a team ranking of soundest attitudes. Each participant should keep a record of his or her own ranking, as well as the team's ranking, for summary and generalization purposes.

Available time is _____.

Step 2: Examining differences between soundest and actual. As a team, review one another's prework rankings. Discuss the reasons for differences between your actual attitude and your team's agreement as to the soundest attitude.

Step 3: Planning for personal behavior change. Write a list of the specific steps you could take to improve your behavior in terms of the soundest attitude toward responsibility in role relationships between student and instructor.

As a team, review one another's action plans and share ways to strengthen personal effectiveness.

Each team will then report its agreed-on ranking. These will be summarized on the blackboard to highlight similarities and differences between teams. The entire group can then examine reasons that may illuminate the source of differences among teams' rankings.

Variations on the Basic Design

Sometimes the clarification of attitudes can proceed only after participants have acquired and reviewed facts and data previously unavailable to them. The basic design can therefore be lengthened to include the introduction of data pertinent to the attitude under study. The design can be interrupted whenever learners are interested in examining factual aspects of the designated topic; for example, after individuals have ranked the alternatives but before teams commit themselves to ranking alternatives for soundness. A TED or TMTD can be used to encourage learners' active exploration and comprehension of the topic.

The following example illustrates how a CAD on the topic of drug use can be coupled with a TED on that subject. Participants complete a multiple-choice attitudes scale as prework, and they also read *Answers to the Most Frequently Asked Questions About Drug Use** and complete a factual multiple-choice test on its contents. Participants then meet in teams assigned on a planned random basis that ensures a wide diversity in membership. The teams follow a TED based on the pamphlet to acquire facts about drugs. They then implement a CAD to arrive at the soundest attitudes toward drug use.

In the following pages, excerpts from the TED multiple-choice test and answer key are followed by an excerpt from the CAD attitude inventory.

How Much Do You Know About Drugs?

Circle the correct answer.

1. Alcohol is
   A. the least dangerous of all drugs.

*Available from Superintendent of Documents, U.S. Government Printing Office, Washington, D.C. 20402.

   B.   a stimulant.
   C.   a depressant.
   D.   has no long-range negative effects.
2. Marijuana
   A.   is a synthetic chemical.
   B.   is a product of the hemp plant.
   C.   is an opium derivative.
   D.   comes from the peyote cactus.
3. The main effect of LSD is
   A.   tension release and relaxation.
   B.   a decrease of painful sensations and drowsiness.
   C.   hallucinatory experiences—sensory experiences such as colors, objects bending, music being "seen."
   D.   a fast increase of energy and release from fatigue.
4. What is the effect of LSD on chromosomes?
   A.   LSD definitely does not have any harmful physiological effects.
   B.   There is no research to suggest LSD breaks chromosomes.
   C.   There is no definite proof that LSD causes chromosome damage.
   D.   LSD definitely causes extensive damage to chromosomes.

Scoring Key and Rationale for Correct Answers

1. C.   Alcohol is a depressant like barbiturates and tranquilizers. Alcoholism is a major drug problem in many countries, including the United States.
2. B.   Marijuana or hashish is derived from the hemp plant. This plant has been cultivated for centuries—both for the drug and for the fiber which is used in making rope.
3. C.   LSD users routinely experience hallucinatory effects as do users of other drugs such as mescaline (from the peyote cactus) and psilocybin (from the Mexican mushroom).
4. C.   Some years ago there was concern that LSD users would have deformed children because of broken

chromosomes. The evidence was of two types. First, people who had taken excessive amounts of LSD had more broken chromosomes than people who had not. Second, in laboratory tests concentrated LSD caused chromosome breakage, visible under a microscope. Subsequent research showed that people evidencing chromosome breakage had taken both large amounts of LSD and many other drugs, most of which were mixed with high proportions of impurities. Other researchers found that concentrated LSD did break chromosomes in the laboratories, but so did concentrated caffeine or aspirin; in other words, the artificially high concentration of the LSD solution, not the LSD itself, broke chromosomes. At present the evidence does not show that LSD causes chromosome damage.

What Are Your Attitudes About Drug Use?

1. Using drugs like marijuana or amphetamines is
   A. a lot of fun that shouldn't be missed.
   B. fun when you get the chance.
   C. okay in moderation.
   D. wrong because these drugs are illegal.
   E. bad because it can lead you to more serious drug use.

Another variation of the design enables the participants to gain an understanding of the attitudes, beliefs, or values of other groups. For example, young people can indicate their attitudes toward different aspects of contemporary living and their perceptions of the attitudes of members of their parents' generation on the same issues. Comparison rankings, obtained from a representative sample of adults, can be used to test the soundness of the younger generation's predictions and the degree of actual divergence in attitudes between the two groups.

Strengths and Limitations

Strengths

A unique advantage of the Clarifying Attitudes Design is that it provides an educational tool that aids learners to clarify their own attitudes, to discuss a spectrum of alternative attitudes, and to consider whether they then want to change their attitudes and corresponding behavior. The design thus facilitates attitude change in a manner that is neither propagandistic nor authoritarian. Because learners are aware of each step in the design and are fully in control of the process, they cannot be covertly influenced or manipulated. Rather, learners freely explore and reason with one another, and their final choices are based on insight and understanding. The design can thus free learners from attitudes that they may have unthinkingly adopted simply because others hold them, and from attitudes that are no longer congruent with the learners' current thinking or with current realities. Learners are not told how they should think or feel, but are expected to carefully articulate their position and exert their best judgment.

Much of the academic, family, business, and social life involves both passive and persuasive interchanges of attitudes, even though these may not be the specific topic of a discussion. Most people are highly interested in learning about the attitudes of others and in expressing their own. The CAD reflects this motivation and provides a structure whereby participants can pursue their natural curiosity concerning others' attitudes and reasoning, and their appreciation of differences between attitudes held by others and their own.

By enabling learners to explore a spectrum of attitudes and hear rationales for them, the design stimulates learners to carefully consider new options and possibilities. Together learners devise a comparison scale to rank the soundest attitude in specific circumstances. These discussions are not only fascinating and provocative but also supportive and constructive applications of social cohesiveness. The team serves not as a locus of blind conformity but as a spur to thoughtfulness and awareness.

Limitations

As discussed earlier in this chapter, only attitudes of a public character, ones that influence individuals' effectiveness and satisfaction, are appropriate for study. Some individuals, however, may have attitudes that appear unconstructive to others but that are also so anchored in their personalities as to be almost impervious to review, comparison, reexamination, or alteration. Attitudes of this magnitude may be accessible to change only by therapy, if at all.

Another set of attitudes may have so little objective or subjective anchorage as to more closely resemble vague feelings, in contrast with attitudes that are relatively crystallized and firmly anchored in facts, data, or logic. These attitudes may also not be readily subject to significant development by the method outlined.

Applications

Learning designs for the examination and evaluation of attitudes have a wide range of applications. Attitudes that have been investigated through the Clarifying Attitudes Design include such issues as work, unions, government, business, children, recreation, politics, education, sex, health, death, political ideologies, and so on.

We can now return to the group of ministers described earlier in this chapter. The attitude inventory they used included the following items:

1. Women and Careers:
   A. People should have the opportunity to work according to their own ability and interests without regard to gender.
   B. Women belong in the home. They are meant to be wives and mothers.
   C. Women and men are different. While we are giving women increased freedom, we must not try to pretend they are the same as men.
   D. Women deserve equal pay and equal opportunities. It's time to lower the barriers against them.
   E. There are biological and traditional differences between women and men that we should respect. People who want to do away with sex roles are playing with fire.

2. Hippies and others who "drop out" of society:
   A. They are basically parasites; they live off the work the rest of us do.
   B. They demonstrate the vitality of the American way of life; they are developing a new ethic for future society.
   C. I have positive feelings about some hippies and negative feelings about others. It depends on the individual person; there are all kinds of hippies.
   D. They are bums who don't want to do their share of work; they should be put in jail and assigned to hard work.
   E. They are young people who are finding themselves and their place in the world. They need time to figure these things out.
3. Sex standards for young people:
   A. Sex is an expression of love and belongs in a close, enduring relationship; marriage is not necessary.
   B. Sex is simply a biological function; there's every reason to experiment with it. Sex can be for showing affection, for fun, or simply for learning how to handle it.
   C. Sex is a natural extension of friendship.
   D. Sex outside of marriage violates the Seventh Commandment; I believe in premarital virginity and marital fidelity.
   E. Sex for young people is not bad in and of itself, but it can lead a young person into situations he or she is not ready for and cannot handle.

As an additional step in this design, the ministers were asked to predict the rank order they thought others in their group would choose. This step allowed them to explore their perceptions of one another. They found, for example, that their individual rankings were significantly more liberal than the rankings they assumed their colleagues would make; that is, each saw the others as more narrow-minded than he felt himself to be. The discovery of this discrepancy permitted them to share their actual attitudes and work toward a more coherent approach to counseling based on a more realistic understanding of one another's views.

7

꩜

The Role of the
Learning Administrator

*Strategies for Strengthening
Team Learning*

꩜ *Learning administrator* is an apt title for a person
who manages learning situations using synergogic designs. A
learning administrator may be a certified teacher or an individual specifically employed to conduct these designs. Not every
certified teacher can immediately become an effective learning
administrator. First he or she must relinquish the idea of a
teacher as someone who is responsible for producing learning
by telling learners information and by giving or withholding rewards in exchange for their compliance and obedience. This
pedagogic orientation contradicts the assumptions implicit in
the designs. The effective learning administrator, therefore, is
one who has no rewards to give or withhold, who may or may
not be a subject-matter expert, and whose activities are limited
to administering a learning process.

Similarly, there are significant differences between the
synergogic learning administrator and the andragogic facilitator.
A key difference concerns the exercise of leadership. In synergogy the designs themselves provide direction and leadership,
with the instructions allowing learners to lead the discussion
and, through critique, to learn from it. In the andragogic model,
the learner is expected to exercise self-initiative, but the teacher

112

assumes the critical role of actively facilitating the learning process. As facilitator, the teacher in the andragogic learning setting assembles subject-matter sources for the learners to study.
Most learners work alone, only occasionally consulting with
others. Even when learning occurs in small groups, the andragogic teacher serves as facilitator. He or she helps learners to
experience a constructive group process by ensuring shared participation, keeping the discussion on the agenda, aiding participants to define and resolve their differences, inviting or providing generalizations as appropriate, and sometimes leading a
critique of group process.

Thus although andragogic teachers do not unilaterally
control the learning experience, but rather tend to share control, their actual or presumed expertise still gives them special
status in the learning process. The learning administrator simply
assists learners in understanding and implementing the design,
and the learners are fully responsible for helping one another to
manage the group process. When andragogic educators who have
acknowledged facilitator skills position themselves as synergogic
learning administrators, they often are struck by how effectively members of small teams can learn without any facilitator.

Thus the teacher trained in pedagogy or andragogy who
wishes to become an effective learning administrator must resist
the temptation to act as an expert or a facilitator. Once learners
understand that synergogy requires them to be active, cooperative, and responsible, the administrator must be careful not to vio-
late these principles. For example, learners should not be encouraged to turn to the expert for help; they must learn to retain
initiative for self-direction and autonomy in achieving goals.

In implementing synergogic designs, the learning administrator fully understands the structure of the learning designs
and the objectives to be achieved from using them. He or she
also appreciates the kinds of student motivations that are relied
upon to spur effort and to promote mutual respect and helpful-
ness within the learning team. Let us examine several distinct
skills that characterize an effective learning administrator. These
concern supporting team effectiveness, supporting individual effectiveness, creating teams, and using subject-matter consultants.

Supporting Effective Team Interaction

Synergogic designs require proactive learners who listen to one another, express their convictions clearly, and do both in such a way as to reach team agreement. To achieve effective team results, members organize themselves to efficiently use the available time, avoid having one or a few individuals dominate the discussion, and implement a number of effective social problem-solving skills. Apart from providing the motivation to learn the topic under study, synergogy enhances the development of skills for personal and social effectiveness, one of the central contributions of this educational approach.

A number of barriers to team action can appear as learners share their knowledge and understanding of facts, information, logic, or attitudes. When an impasse is reached, the learning administrator may need to intervene in a way that brings the problem to the attention of team members and allows them to resolve the impasse, and at the same time encourages them to learn to identify and resolve *future* team-action problems. The learning administrator seeks to contribute such instruction without establishing authoritarian control over students; he or she intervenes only when a team seems unable to work out how they will work together.

Among the more important causes of impasse within learning teams are:

- win-lose fighting among team members
- inability to reach consensus because one individual holds out for an answer that others refuse to endorse
- personal antagonisms that preclude reasoned argument
- inability to restrain a member who talks too much
- inability to involve the reticent learner who talks too little

Any one of these process problems can hamper effective team action. Progress is slowed if members devote an undue amount of time to these issues at the expense of the subject matter. Particularly with learners new to the use of synergogic designs, such difficulties are likely to repeatedly arise.

An observer might at first wonder if synergogic designs are unsatisfactory because they can occasion negative behavior or wheel spinning. But upon consideration, one realizes that these kinds of difficulties also hinder employed adults in their interactions at work. Perhaps, then, learners in high school, college, and the workplace need to gain experience in learning how to resolve such difficulties, particularly when this experience comes in the process of acquiring knowledge, attitudes, or skills. Thus teamwork skills are no less important than the learning objectives associated with the content of a particular design.

The question facing the learning administrator is how to intervene so that participants learn team skills, but without either telling them what to do or becoming a facilitator.

Deciding Whether to Intervene

The decision about whether or not to intervene is the initial issue, with the kind of intervention of secondary consideration. In deciding whether to intervene, a learning administrator might ponder the following questions:

- Is the problem serious enough to require an intervention, or should the learners solve it themselves?
- Does the team have enough remaining time to resolve the problem through critique?
- Would intervention help silent members, who are presently being ignored, to express their thoughts and feelings?
- Would intervention motivate the team to work harder or better?

If an administrator is leaning toward an intervention, he or she should also consider these questions:

- If I intervene, should I explain *why* I'm doing it or just do it?
- Can I intervene in such a way as to ensure that the team retains responsibility for handling the problem, or do I risk making the team feel defeated?

- Can I intervene in such a way as to solve the problem while aiding the team members to maintain or increase their self-respect?
- Can I provide examples or an illustration so that participants will understand exactly what I am suggesting?

Regardless of the particular interaction problem, the learning administrator should intervene only if the problem is sufficiently signficant; control should not be exercised under the guise of being helpful. For example, an effective learning administrator does *not*: appoint a discussion leader or a secretary; interrupt when in disagreement with what is being said, or on hearing a misstatement of fact; enter the discussion as a guest team member to state an opinion or give hints; act as timekeeper, parliamentarian, or disciplinarian.

In the typical team that is starting a synergogic design for the first time, the learning administrator may observe that participants immediately start to work on the task without discussing how they will use their time or how much agreement will serve as the standard for answering a question. While the ensuing discussion is likely to be spirited, the results are also likely to be of low quality. This places a premium on critique, which allows learners to begin to plan how to work together on the next activity. The learning administrator need not intervene just because the quality of this discussion is poor. If he or she does not intervene, it will become apparent that the learners themselves are highly motivated to solve the problem of how to work better. Intervention is introduced only when learner-centered facilitation has reached an impasse.

A learning administrator may be concerned at first that the discussion will slide off the topic, that team discipline is insufficient, or that loud voices mean destructive dispute. None of these are true. Learners may stand up, mill around, or lean in their chairs, but such activity does not necessarily indicate boredom, frustration, or tension; rather some learners need to work off their excess energy, and others act this way when they are trying to express themselves. A clear understanding of designs, along with well-tested observations of the team's actions, should enable the learning administrator to develop an understanding of when and how to proceed with an intervention.

Deciding How to Intervene

Consider the following situations typical of those faced by a learning administrator. Before reading the recommended strategy, you may want to consider how you would react.

Time-keeping. Early in a team discussion of a multiple-choice test, one of the team members turns to you and asks, "What time do we have to be finished?" What would you say?

Restate the schedule and remind the team that they should finish on time. You could also note that they can refer to the printed schedule for guidance.

Defining terms. During a critique of team interactions, one of the teams is unable to decide how to define terms used in the discussion of decision making, such as *majority thinking* or *consensus.* A member turns to you and asks, "Would you define these terms for us?" What would you do?

Refrain from offering a dictionary definition. The team needs to define these terms in relationship to the team process that has led to their indecision. Point out that the issue is already under discussion in the team and that they should attempt to resolve it. Also invite discussion of this problem in general session.

Skipping steps. After completing team scoring, a team begins its critique before consulting the rationale sheets for the key. What would you do?

Call the team's attention to the rationale sheets because they may have been overlooked. Explain that they are part of the design, intended to give teams an opportunity to improve their understanding. But, leave it to their discretion whether to use the rationale.

Absent teams. It is time to begin the scoring in general

session of a Team Effectiveness Design. All teams are present but one. What would you do?

The learning administrator should begin the activity on time. Any delay serves only to penalize the teams who are present on time. When late members arrive, they will find themselves at a disadvantage and will experience pressure from their colleagues to be on time for future activities.

Monitoring. You are about to enter a team room in a normal monitoring round, but find the door locked. What would you do?

Intervene by knocking on the door, and ask the team to leave the door unlocked. If members are uncomfortable with monitoring or observation, their reservations should be discussed and resolved. Finally, explain to the team that you, as learning administrator, are responsible for monitoring teams to ensure quality.

Split decision. A team has spent one hour discussing procedure and is evenly split into two sides and is unable to move on. What would you do?

Intervene. Try to help them back away from procedural concerns to examine the reasons for their disagreement.

Improvised rules. You go to the team room and see Joe, a member of the team, in the hallway reading a newspaper. You ask him if the team is taking a break and he says, "No, they are critiquing my refusal to agree and I decided it would be better for them to talk freely, without me there to embarrass them." What would you do?

Point out that his absence may be unproductive, that he will probably not be able to openly and usefully respond to his teammates if he does not understand their reasoning. Ask the team to include Joe in its discussions, since much of the value of the task is in Joe hearing the discussion.

Supporting Individual Effectiveness

Sometimes teams encounter problems that result from an individual's attitude or performance, and the team may not have the resources for coping with them. Four of the most typical such problems are chronic low preparation, inappropriate attitudes, excessive dependency, and attrition. In each case, the learning administrator can help by talking privately with the learner. Problems resulting from team interactions, however, should be left to the team or addressed by a team intervention.

Poor Individual Preparation

Problems of poor preparation are likely to be short-lived because learners quickly come to realize that adequate preparatory work is prerequisite to participation. Learners who have had many courses in which preparation played a negligible role will usually correct themselves as they gain experience with the synergogic approach.

If a participant refuses to study, the learning administrator must address the person directly. A participant in a voluntary activity can be asked to enroll at a later time, when he or she will be able to complete the preparation. Or the member may be asked to excuse him or herself from team and general meetings until the preparation has been done.

If an individual's fundamental qualifications to participate are insufficient to allow constructive interaction with others at the same level, the learning administrator should reexamine whether other less-demanding academic situations might not be more appropriate.

Poor Attitudes Toward Participation

If a course is nonvoluntary, some participants may have poor attitudes toward participation. In academic settings, for example, some students want to pass the course but by doing as little as possible. In corporate settings, individuals who are required to attend training courses whose purpose they do not understand or do not see as relevant, or courses whose schedules are inconvenient, may resent being expected to participate. Some may have insufficient time for preparation due to other obligations; others may fear that personal information that surfaces during sessions will be reported back to supervisors. A

host of similar concerns not related to learning itself can provoke resentment. Such resentment may take the form of poor
preparation, ineffective team contributions, refusal to actively
participate, or disrupting other team members by being overly
argumentative or by clowning.

When a participant is showing signs of indifference or
hostility, the learning administrator should attempt to talk to
that individual privately. Sometimes the airing of personal reactions and feelings about issues not directly associated with the
learning designs can be useful. For example, the opportunity to
talk privately may allow a participant to explain why the learning activities seem overly taxing or foolish. The learning administrator may then be able to aid the participant to reassess his or
her unconstructive attitudes and adopt more effective ones. If
such intervention fails, the individual may need counseling,
which the learning administrator should not be expected to provide. In an academic setting, specialist services may be available;
in other cases the only practical solution is likely to be time.

Excessive Dependency

Some individuals are extremely dependent on having an
authority figure to provide guidance, rewards for compliance,
and discipline for noncompliance. When placed in a situation in
which they must exercise freedom and self-responsibility for
learning, they feel threatened and insecure. Some interpret the
absence of an authority figure as the withholding of necessary
help and do not see how they are to proceed. Others feel socially incompetent to participate in a give and take with colleagues.
These learners may view the synergogic design as exposing their
incompetencies, which increases their anxiety and desire for
protection. But if the learning administrator responds to these
needs in hopes of reducing such anxiety, the potential strengths
of the synergogic designs are largely reduced.

Instead, the learning administrator might recombine
teams. Or the learning administrator could use pedagogic strategies with the dependent learner rather than pressing the learner
to continue to participate in something for which he or she is

not adequately competent. Such activity would not remedy the learner's dependency problem, of course, but it would enable him or her to continue studying the subject matter. This means providing the learner access to outside help of the sort that many school systems or industrial organizations are prepared to supply, such as counseling, coaching, or subject-matter expertise. This help may be supplemental to synergogic learning or in place of it.

Attrition

At times individuals may find it necessary to leave a course for legitimate organizational or personal reasons. But dropping a course is sometimes a way to avoid a learning situation rather than coping with it. The learning administrator should make an effort to determine the departing learner's reasons and feelings. If the problem's source concerns the team, they may be able to resolve it in a way that enables the learner to continue. The participant should not be forced to remain but should stay only if his or her convictions support that decision.

Creating Teams

The learning administrator also has to make decisions regarding team composition. Four basic issues arise in such determinations: (1) Should teams be homogeneous or heterogeneous in terms of learners' skills, interests, age, sex, or other factors? (2) Through how many repetitions of a given design are teams kept intact? (3) How many members should teams have? (4) Can self-nomination or sociometric choice be the basis for team assignments? Let us examine each of these issues in turn.

Homogeneity and Heterogeneity

Composing teams on a homogeneous basis—that is, putting people together who are alike according to qualifications, approach, or other matching aspects—is likely to be useful when the learning goal is for all members to have relatively equal opportunity to think, analyze, and learn. For example, for a TED or TMTD that involves mathematics, the learners with the greatest mathematical skill would be placed on the same team or teams, those with moderate competence on other teams, and those with the least mathematical competence on still other teams. Each team proceeds at its own pace—the most-competent learners need not slow down to accommodate slower learners, and the least-competent learners do not have to struggle to keep up with the more advanced. While in absolute terms the least-competent learners may not learn as much as the highly competent ones, they may learn *relatively* more by being grouped according to their ability.

For other designs, however, *heterogeneous* teaming will yield teams whose participants represent a range of individual differences. Such diversity may be useful if the design concerns a controversial topic that should be examined from many viewpoints.

Thus the learning administrator appraises the learner population and identifies those aspects most crucial to the subject matter *and* social learning gains desired. At this point, one or more particular team arrangements may suggest themselves. If it seems likely that an arrangement will produce a moderate gain in subject matter or skill learning but will interfere with previously established positive social-learning trends, the learning administrator can informally apply a "mini-max" criterion, selecting the arrangement that will provide maximum individual subject- or skill-learning and minimum social disruption.

Similar considerations are involved in deciding whether to have learning teams composed on a single-sex basis or on a mixed basis. Under certain circumstances, competition between single-sex teams provides additional motivation, presuming that other bases of team composition are equal. Alternation of single-sex and mixed-team arrangements may add variety and give learners opportunities to refine their interaction skills in both kinds of settings.

Changing Teams

The learning administrator decides whether to keep the same team membership through successive learning tasks. Again, the overall goals of the course determine this choice. If the goal is for individuals to be effective in team learning, membership may need to be changed so that teamwork skills are distributed fairly evenly through the study teams. While the initial distribution may have been adequate when the teams were first composed, as participants interact and work in their teams, some teams may become noticeably more zestful and effective, and others run out of energy. Still later, interteam disparities may lessen or widen. The skilled learning administrator develops a sense of when, on the basis of monitoring observations, it is time to recompose team memberships. Whether early or late in the sequence, it is desirable that each team have at least one person whose effectiveness as a team member is high. Then others benefit from his or her contribution to their effectiveness, and at the same time they can learn from that person's example how to be more effective themselves.

Size

Synergogic designs can be used with teams of two to ten learners. The key consideration is that the larger the number of learners in a study team, the less amount of time available for active participation by each individual. However, if learning benefits can be gained simply by listening to others, little is lost by having large teams. But if the learning benefits are gained only through the process of participation, the teams should be relatively small.

For a wide range of subject matter, study teams of five or six are ideal. If the number of learners is fewer than five, there is the possibility of inadequate intellectual stimulation, as too few points of view are presented. With more than six members, some points of view may fail to get an adequate hearing, since each individual has less time to make a case.

Self-Selection

Voluntarism and choice as to teammates can be an important source of motivation and can promote better teamwork. When class members do not know one another well enough to make choices, the learning administrator can provide criteria that allow each person to volunteer for a particular team. The criteria may be based on sex—some same-sex and some mixed teams—or based on age, experience, and the like.

When classmates know one another, sociometric preferences can be employed for creating teams. Each participant lists those with whom he or she would prefer to be teamed. These preferences are honored as best as possible by the learning administrator, who treats the preferences as confidential and arranges the teams. Although some learners will be more popular than others, most will have a few friends with whom they prefer to be associated.

Self-nomination and sociometric choosing seem to be more important to grade school and college students than to adult learners. These ways may be utilized when no explicit basis for assignment pertains to the learning result.

Using Subject-Matter Consultants

If the learning administrator is not an expert in the subject matter under study, he or she can arrange for a subject-matter consultant to meet with the class, although this is not always necessary or desirable. The consultant would meet with students to explore subtleties, test out implications, or strengthen generalizations. When doing so, the consultant acts as a collaborator and not as a lecturer. This is practicable once the learners have achieved insight into the subject based on learner-centered designs.

8

⊶⌇⌁⌁⌇⌁⌁⌇⌁⌁⌇⌁

Applications
in Business Settings

⊶⌁⌁ On-the-job training and development programs are based on the assumption that the better an employee's knowledge, attitudes, and skills, the less supervision he or she will require in making an effective contribution to the organization's performance. In other words, the more a person knows about the tasks at hand, the greater his or her capacity for self-direction. In this chapter, we examine the ways in which synergogic designs can be used to support improved organization performance by considering the topic of safety training as an example. Any number of organization practices and problems, however, can be addressed by training and development courses using synergogic designs.

Safety

Safety in potentially hazardous situations is one of the most complex of modern problems in the workplace, in part because of the increasing complexity of modern plants, facilities, and equipment, and the regulations pertaining to them. The most-frequent causes of accidents are mechanical and operator error. Accidents result from poorly designed equipment that is unreliable; equipment that requires overly complex skills on the part of the operator; faulty electronic feedback systems that do not give critical information to the operator; inadequate training of the operator; and operator error due to accident proneness, subtle incapacitation (which refers to the operator appear-

125

ing to be alert to emerging risks but in fact being unable to respond in a timely manner), or unsafe attitudes.

   Viewed in a broad way, safety is the joint result of knowledge, attitude, and skill. Knowledge of rules for proper operation and use of equipment, skill in using tools, and a watchful
and cautious attitude toward safety—all contribute to the degree of safety or danger in a given situation. When these factors
are present, safety will be significantly improved; in the absence
of any one factor, accidents are more likely. Yet other influ-
ences on safety result from the organization's practices and
structure; for example, the manner in which authority is exercised, whether safety inspection is a regular part of everyone's
duties or is the concern only of the official inspectors, and
whether safety rules are routinely disregarded by supervisory
personnel and others.

   Because of the importance of safety, it is a high priority
for organizations, and they should use the most effective educational practices to increase safety. In this chapter we present
three situations in which safety training is approached using
synergogic designs. The first concerns safety on the plant floor,
such as in a construction area, a refinery, a chemical plant, or
other similar manufacturing locations. The second example addresses safety in the cockpit of the modern jet airliner; the third
application, safety procedures in the practice of medicine. In
each of these areas, all four synergogic designs are employed to
aid persons who are at risk to develop more knowledge, better
skills, or more positive attitudes—all related to improving safety.

Safety in the Manufacturing Plant

   This illustration is drawn from a training program for new
employees who received two hours of training a day during
their first month of work in a manufacturing plant. The safety
segment occurred near the end of the training course.

TED for Knowledge Acquisition

   During one of the formal sessions, each participant is provided with the company safety manual, which discusses the set-

ting and use of personal safety equipment, emergency procedures for sounding an alarm, use of fire protection and fire-
extinguishing equipment, and other plant-wide issues, as contrasted with specific safe practices on a given job. After reading
the material, each individual completes a factual multiple-choice
test on its contents. At the next session each learning team
works together to decide the single best answer to each of the
questions. For example, three questions concerned with the
best way to put out or contain a fire are:

1. Water is the best way of putting out
   A. burning oil.
   B. a wood fire.
   C. an electrical fire.
   D. a magnesium fire.
2. CO_2 is useful for putting out a fire when the source is
   A. burning grease.
   B. paper.
   C. electrical appliances.
   D. metal.
3. It is dangerous to make any attempt to put out a fire whose
   source is
   A. alcohol.
   B. magnesium.
   C. electrical wiring.
   D. hydrogen sulfide.

[*Correct answers:* 1 (B), 2 (A), 3 (D).]

As part of a second TED learning design, participants
view a film of the plant in operation. The film includes some
twenty-five hazardous situations that were actually observed
during the filming. Participants are asked to record all the
examples of hazardous or unsafe situations and practices that
they can recognize. Then the teams view the film, score team
observations, and study the answer key and rationale. The film
is replayed and followed by further team discussion. Finally,
each learning team tours a designated section of the plant to
uncover potentially hazardous conditions and make recommendations for correcting them.

CAD for Improving Attitudes

Although individuals may be aware of safe practices and alert to hazardous circumstances, accidents may continue to occur if any individuals have lax or careless attitudes toward safety. Thus the plant's safety training program includes an exercise intended to help participants develop a shared attitude of common concern for one another's safety.

Each participant is asked to rank order a set of attitude statements concerning safety. First, they are to rank items from the soundest attitude—the one most likely to promote an accident-free work place—to the least sound. Second, they are to rank the same items but from the one most characteristic or typical of actual conditions in the plant to the least characteristic. For example:

1. Safety programs should be implemented by
    A. a safety committee of representatives from all departments.
    B. a safety director who is responsible to step in "on the spot" to improve safety.
    C. employee relations personnel since they have the best overall view of all employees.
    D. all employees.
    E. line supervision, since they are accountable for their subordinates' safety.
2. Protective equipment at our plant is
    A. provided at great expense to the company and reflects management's concern for people.
    B. mandatory in some areas, with the line supervisor responsible for its use.
    C. very cumbersome to wear and, therefore, can cause more accidents than it prevents.
    D. not critical to wear, but exposure to accidents is possible if it is not used.
    E. provided for the health and safety of the employees with responsibility for proper use up to each person.

3. When a person is not wearing eye protection in a safety
   goggle area you should
   A. do nothing because the person must have a reason for
   not wearing it.
   B. make a note and bring it up at the next safety meeting.
   C. report it to the supervisor as soon as possible.
   D. point out that this is an eye protection area and make
   your concern known.
   E. ignore it, because this person believes he or she knows
   the job best and will resent your interference.

During the team discussion the two ranking procedures
are repeated, and teams exchange their agreed-on conclusions.
Next, participants discuss specific actions each could undertake
to increase the safety of the plant. In a general session each
team reports its conclusions.

Safety in the Jet Airliner Cockpit

More than any other single activity of modern industry,
the airliner cockpit has received careful analysis of the conditions essential to safe operation. Such attention is essential because a crash could involve several hundred fatalities and serious
injuries. Today's pilots must be proficient fliers and expert managers, for captains are responsible for both the technical components and personnel in the cockpit. Thus a captain needs special
leadership, management skills, and knowledge in the event of a
crisis. In the cockpit, any lack of coordination among the crew
or insubordination could have fatal consequences.

When confronted with a crisis, a captain may think it best
to exercise decisiveness by formulating a plan and insisting on
its execution. Such decisiveness, the captain might presume, will
command the confidence of the crew, reduce the likelihood of
faulty coordination, and minimize the risk of insubordination.
However, such decisiveness could also prevent the captain from
receiving the kind of information critical to a more valid definition of the problem or from considering alternatives and options that might further reduce the risk. Ideally, then, a captain

must deal with a crisis in such a way as to induce confidence, elicit cooperation, and at the same time allow other crew members to contribute their resources for problem definition and problem solving.

The synergogic approach to cockpit safety involves a series of designs. First, captains and other crew study alternative styles of exercising leadership during a crisis or uncertainty and develop the skills needed to implement their new concept of leadership.

Knowledge

As prework all participants in the seminar study the text *Cockpit Resource Management.** They then complete a Team Effectiveness Design to assess their understanding of the factual information in the text. The design requires members to use their skills of inquiry and advocacy, both of which are essential to finding creative solutions to emergencies in the cockpit. Additionally, the activities test participants' abilities to cooperate effectively in pooling their knowledge and reaching valid team decisions. The synergogic design provides a high degree of realism and highlights the need for team members to take advantage of everyone's input to discover the soundest approach prior to making a decision.

Attitudes

Participants next individually complete the rank ordering of several attitude statements concerned with cockpit resource management. For example, one item asks them to rank order from most effective to least effective these five types of leadership styles:

A. The captain seeks to establish a warm and friendly atmosphere in the cockpit. This minimizes the need to exercise

*R. R. Blake, J. S. Mouton, and United Airlines Command/Leadership/Resource Management Steering Committee and Working Groups, *Cockpit Resource Management* (Denver, Colo., and Austin, Tex.: Cockpit Resource Management, 1982).

authority. Agreements come in an easy way since there is cohesion among crew members.

B. The captain exercises authority so as to maintain a balance between the needs for effective performance and the desires of other crew members. He retains responsibility for ultimate decisions but understands that it is important to take the views of others into account.

C. The captain rarely exercises authority as for the most part the flight operates itself. Other crew members offer relevant information if necessary.

D. The captain feels accountable only to himself. Since the responsibility is his, he expects his decisions to be accepted as final. He asks for information from the other crew members only when necessary.

E. The captain makes effective use of authority by directing the effort in such a manner as to maximize crew involvement and participation. In this way he gains the use of all available resources toward the objective of excellence. When time is a critical factor he does not hesitate to decide or choose a course of action.

Each team then meets to formulate a consensus ranking for the soundest leadership style. Uniformly, teams using this design select alternative E as the most effective style. In a general session, all teams further discuss this alternative, which further reinforces their convictions.

Skills

Having used the CAD to establish criteria for effective leadership, each captain has two opportunities to demonstrate his or her effectiveness in managing crew resources through a Performance Judging Design. During the first activity one third of the participants are designated captains, the others as crew members. Each captain is confronted with two comparable emergencies, each with two different crew members. For example, captain A confronts emergency 1 with crew members B and C. Captain D solves a similar problem with crew members E and F. Then, emergency 2 is solved by captain A with crew

members E and F, while captain D solves emergency with crew
A and B. Each crew member then evaluates the performance of
captains A and D, judging which was the most effective.

A typical emergency problem consists of a description
given to each of the crew members (paragraph A). However, the
first and second officer each receive additional information unknown to the captain (paragraphs B and C, respectively). Each
captain has fifteen minutes to determine the most effective action to take.

Paragraph A

You are on a scheduled flight that was des-
tined for Salt Lake City (SLC), an airport in the
western U.S. located in a high valley with higher
peaks immediately to the east. Airport elevation is
4200 meters above sea level. There was a weather
delay and you held for one-half hour awaiting an
approach, which used up most of your holding
fuel. You are now en route to your alternate, Boise,
Idaho (BOI), which is approximately 250 nautical
miles northwest of Salt Lake City. The weather at
Boise is reported as 2 miles visibility with drizzle
and poor braking, wind calm. As your aircraft approaches the Boise area, you receive word that a
DC-8, which has just landed, has missed a taxiway
and its nosewheel is buried in deep mud and par-
tially collapsed. Most of the aircraft is protruding
across the runway near its midpoint 4500 feet
down the runway. This aircraft cannot be cleared
from the runway for at least one to one and a half
hours. The other runway at Boise is closed due to
construction and has several ditches dug across it.

All other airports within your fuel range are
zero-zero (WOXOF), except SLC, which is still below landing minimums, with RVR 1200 variable
to RVR 1000. There is a 15-knot crosswind and
the weather is slowly deteriorating. You have 90
minutes of fuel remaining. You are 45 minutes
from Salt Lake City and 10 minutes from Boise.

Paragraph B

It appears to you that the options are to attempt a landing on the restricted runway in Boise, with poor braking; or to make a landing in below minimum weather and strong crosswind at Salt Lake City. From previous experience, you feel that this particular aircraft can be stopped safely under the existing conditions at Boise on the runway available. At the very worst, a landing at Boise would require steering off the runway at very low speed if it appeared you could not stop completely before reaching the disabled DC-8.

All things considered, it seems to you that the better course of action is to land at Boise.

Paragraph C

A fear you have is that the captain of this flight usually carries excessive airspeed at touchdown on landings. His approaches have always been excellent and very precise, but he always carries excess airspeed. His normal profile over the end of the runway, while always precise is normally very fast, causing touchdowns to be frequently well down the runway. This has caused no problems in the past because of the length of the runways you have been landing on. You feel this captain would have no problem in making a successful approach and landing at Salt Lake City even if there is a strong crosswind and the weather is below minimums. However, you seriously doubt that the captain could successfully stop the aircraft on the short runway surface available at Boise, particularly with the poor braking reported at Boise. You are worried that the aircraft would not even be slowed appreciably before reaching the DC-8.

Several years ago during a landing under similar conditions, you experienced hydroplaning and the aircraft traveled a great distance on the runway with very little deceleration even though everything possible was being done to stop it.

You will, therefore, strongly advocate returning to Salt Lake City unless you are completely convinced that a landing at Boise is the better option. You do not feel you should explicitly mention the captain's excessive speed on approach as you do not want to make him defensive and unreceptive to your suggestions.

The crews then fly training flights in the airplane simulator and these are videotaped. These simulator flights pose several hazards that test crew members' safety skills. The crew members view the tapes and spend two or more hours critiquing their performance, again using instruments for evaluating leadership and teamwork.

The conclusion reached by simulator instructors is that neither a simulator instructor nor any other licensed flyer who is not a member of the crew is an acceptable source of feedback. Only feedback from the actual crew contributes effectively to learning. Trained crews that have been evaluated by Federal Aviation Administration proficiency checks have been found to conduct even routine missions with significantly fewer mistakes, suggesting that the synergogic approach to training is making practical contributions to in-flight safety.

Safety in the Practice of Medicine

Among the safety issues of concern to medical professionals are those related to legal liability. Various laws, whose interpretations depend on judicial rulings and precedents, offer certain protections to both the medical practitioner and the patient. In recent years, for example, the concept of patient consent has been refined and reinterpreted. Medical professionals, therefore, need to keep abreast of the intricacies of new legal rulings with regard to the degree of risk involved in various kinds of medical decisions. They need the opportunity to think through the more common sources of risk in order to be able to exercise mature judgment in cases that pose complex liability issues.

Such training would be fairly simple if a medical authority or an expert on medical ethics could simply recite to medical practitioners a complete list of hypothetical situations and the correct response to each. But neither the practice of medicine nor the subtleties of the relevant law permit such solutions. Furthermore, in cases involving patient consent relevant factors include the practitioner's interpretation of the patient's actions as implying consent and the patient's presumptions as to his or her own responsibilities in agreeing to a medical intervention. Thus the practitioner's knowledge of the law must be supplemented by various interpretive skills and judgmental abilities.

Several synergogic designs have been employed to enable medical practitioners to better understand issues of liability and malpractice.

Knowledge

A Team Effectiveness Design is based on participants' reading of *The Doctor and the Law,** particularly chapter 7, which discusses the relationship between law and medical practice. After reading the text, participants individually complete a five-alternative multiple-choice test that focuses on the major issues in the designated text. Three sample questions are:

1. Consent for examination or treatment requires that the patient
   A. be given enough information for him to make a judgment.
   B. be asked to sign an appropriate consent form.
   C. have all risks and advantages explained to him.
   D. be allowed time to discuss the matter with friends.
   E. be informed about the various components of the planned maneuver.

---

*J. L. Taylor, *The Doctor and the Law*, 2nd ed. (London: Pitman, 1982).

2. It is generally advisable to obtain written consent for
    A. normal investigation procedures.
    B. standard treatment regimes involving the use of dan-
        gerous substances.
    C. operations requiring general anesthesia.
    D. diagnostic or treatment procedures carried out on chil-
        dren.
    E. treatment procedures for persons detained in mental
        hospitals.
3. When surgery is contemplated for sterilizing a patient it is
    A. highly desirable to discuss the operation with the
        spouse.
    B. obligatory for the consent form to be countersigned
        by the spouse.
    C. very desirable for the form to be signed by the patient.
    D. not obligatory for the spouse to countersign the pa-
        tient's consent.
    E. up to the spouse to raise legal objections.

The practitioners bring their prework to the seminar and
work in teams to agree on answers to the test. The TED continues with analysis of the answer key and rationale. Team and
individual score comparisons are made to give participants a
measure of how they worked together and what they learned
from one another. During a general seminar the participants
move beyond the specifics of the material studied to probe the
implications of what they have learned.

Applying Knowledge

A second TED requires participants to draw conclusions
based on the factual information acquired in the first design.
The multiple-choice questions in this second TED demand
thoughtful and subtle reasoning, and for any question more
than one alternative may be correct. For example:

1. A doctor's action would appear to constitute assault
    A. when a patient signs a form permitting him to perform
        an operation and the operation is not successful.

B.   in the course of a routine examination, a doctor, with-
     out saying anything, lances a large boil on the patient's
     back.

C.   a patient agrees wholly to a blood test; the doctor's
     hand slips and the needle injures the patient.

D.   a surgeon mistakenly believes that his staff have ob-
     tained consent for the herniorrhaphy he performs on a
     patient.

E.   a patient's life is in danger; the doctor asks permission
     to administer treatment; the patient refuses on reli-
     gious grounds; the physician proceeds and saves the
     patient's life.

2.   A patient requests treatment for two boils. The doctor tells
     the patient that he is going to lance the boils. The patient
     orally agrees. After the first boil has been lanced the pa-
     tient complains of pain. He tells the doctor not to lance the
     second boil. The doctor warns of the danger of letting the
     second one go untreated; the patient closes his eyes and
     holds up his arm; the doctor lances the second boil. Subse-
     quently, a secondary infection develops where the second
     boil was lanced and the patient sues the doctor for assault.

     The most likely court finding or findings is that

A.   the subsequent infection of the boil is a critical factor
     in determining liability for assault.

B.   the patient's telling the physician not to lance the sec-
     ond boil could not overrule his initial consent.

C.   the doctor is not liable because of the patient's ex-
     pressed consent.

D.   the doctor is not liable because the patient's action im-
     plied consent.

E.   the doctor is liable.

3.   In which of the following situations does the doctor have
     consent to give treatment which has not been given by the
     words or actions of the patient.

A.   A patient has fallen down and suffered a blow on the
     head; he is bleeding profusely from the mouth and
     nose; he is conscious but in deep shock.

B.   A person who is bleeding from surface cuts on his arm
     walks into the doctor's surgery.

C.   A doctor discovers multiple fibroids in the uterus of
     his anesthetized patient during an appendectomy.
D.   An accident victim with a broken back is conscious but
     extremely intoxicated.

Answer and rationale for item 1. B, D, and E constitute
assault because (1) no emergency exists to legitimatize unilat-
eral action on the doctor's part and (2) the patient was not consulted (B and D) or refused permission (E). The law has always
required the physician to obtain the consent of the patient to
treatment. Consent to general treatment of the school of medicine of the physician's training is implied from the conduct of
the patient in seeking out the physician in the first instance. Beyond this, however, the law has always required specific consent
by the patient to all operative procedures. Otherwise, the procedure, however beneficial to the patient, constitutes an assault
and battery by the physician upon the person of the patient,
rendering the physician liable to the patient without proof of
negligence. It has also long been the law that consent to be valid
and binding must be an informed consent, that is, the consenter
must be aware of what it is he or she is being asked to consent to.

Answer and rationale for item 2. D is correct because
consent may be either expressed or implied.

Answer and rationale for item 3. A and D are correct because expressed consent is not necessary when the patient is
either injured or unconscious and prompt attention is reasonably necessary for the preservation of life or limb. C is correct
because a surgeon should be entitled to follow sound medical
practice in extending an operation when the advisability of
additional surgery becomes apparent during the course of an
operation. There are certain risks inherent in anesthesia and surgery, which are always present, even in routine surgery. Subject-
ing a patient to a second operation, with its attendant risks and
costs, merely for the purpose of first obtaining a consent that
the patient would give anyway, if he were conscious, is uncon-
scionable. In the absence of clearly specific prohibitions on the
part of the patient, the physician should be privileged to perform such surgery within the operative field as is justified in
prevailing medical opinion.

The design continues with team identification of the correct answers, during which participants share their reasoning about correct and incorrect answers. Teams score their answers, receiving 3 points for every correct answer and deducting 3 points for every incorrect answer. This arrangement thus introduces penalties for the wrong judgment and also for missing a correct answer. Teams also compare their learning efficiency rates.

A subsequent general seminar discussion is led by an expert in medical ethics. However, the expert does not lecture on the subject matter; rather, he or she responds to questions and explains the relevant rationale or legal precedents.

Skills

The following example illustrates a Performance Judging Design intended to help practitioners reduce the risks inherent in the practice of medicine. Participants read the case study as prework and then meet in teams to consider the implications of the incident, discuss the solution and prevention of the specific problem, and extract principles for future application.

The Cut Hand

Tuesday evenings were usually quiet in the emergency room but tonight was very different. By 9:00 P.M. Dr. John Clark had seen three cases that could, and should, have been dealt with by family doctors. Instead, the young man and two children had been brought to the hospital "to save calling our doctor." Staff Nurse Jones was sympathetic and, like Dr. Clark, she was new to the department. She thought it was unreasonable for the staff to be bothered "at this time of night by other people's troubles."

There had been an interesting case earlier in the evening. It was a classic Colles fracture in a middle-aged woman. Because they were busy, Dr. Clark had referred her to someone else.

It had been a long day and Dr. Clark was about to return to the staff residence to relax when Mr James Campbell was brought into the emergency room by a friend. They had been drinking in a nearby bar and, according to the patient, during an expansive movement of his right hand, he had knocked over a stemmed glass at the bar and cut the back of his hand. As though seeking sympathy, he said, "It was half full too."

The hand was wrapped up in a wet, blood-stained handkerchief. The cut was clean, vertical, one inch long on the dorsum of the right hand between the extensor tendons of the index and middle fingers. After cleaning the wound, Dr. Clark was able to confirm that there was no particular bleeding point, only oozing; the extensor tendons were intact and there was no evidence of loss of sensation in the fingers. He confirmed the tetanus immunization state of the patient and arranged for him to be given toxoid.

"Alright, Doc! Sew it up and let's get back to the party."

Dr. Clark infiltrated both edges of the wound with local anesthetic and closed the wound with three interrupted sutures. In conversation he found out that Mr. Campbell was a visitor to the area and was expecting to return home the following evening. He reassured Mr. Campbell about the injury and advised him to make an appointment with his own doctor in seven days' time for removal of the sutures. In the usual way, he added, "and if you are troubled by it in the next twenty-four hours, come back."

He completed the record card as follows:

> Cut dorsum (R) hand 1"
> Clean - tendons intact
> Stitch × 3 TT
> See own GP 7/7   J.C.

In the meantime, another case was brought into the emergency and Staff Nurse Jones invited Dr. Clark to look at an eye injury.

Six weeks later Dr. Clark received a message to report to

the hospital administrator's office. There he was shown the following letter from a lawyer:

> Dear Sir,
>
> We are writing this letter in behalf of Mr. James Campbell of 26 High Street, Middletown, Massachusetts.
>
> Mr. Campbell was brought to the emergency room of your hospital suffering from a laceration to the back of his hand. He was treated by your emergency room personnel and three stitches were inserted. He returned to your hospital four days later and requested that the stitches be removed. He was told that this could not be done at the hospital, as it was not the hospital's task to remove stitches. Accordingly, Mr. Campbell, on his return home, visited his own doctor who removed the stitches. The hand was still swollen and our client's doctor removed a small piece of glass from the surface of the scab.
>
> After another twelve days the swelling of our client's hand had subsided and the scar was healing, but there was a lump on his hand. He revisited his own doctor, who diagnosed that a piece of glass had been left in the hand when the wound was originally sutured. Accordingly, on the next morning our client visited a local hospital for treatment. The presence of a piece of glass in the wound showed up clearly on the x ray. Our client was at the hospital from 9:00 A.M. until 2:30 P.M., and during that period he spent almost three hours in the operating theater under a local anesthetic. A piece of glass was removed with difficulty and a drain was inserted in the wound. This was removed the following day and the stitches were finally removed a week later.
>
> We are awaiting an up-to-date medical report on our client's condition.

On these facts our client has undoubtedly a claim of negligence against your hospital and against the medical personnel who was in charge of the emergency room. We write to give you notice accordingly and would ask you to put us in touch with the hospital insurers and for you to provide us with the full name of your emergency room and the medical person who was in charge.

Individual prework. Based on the facts of this case, answer the following question: What are you going to do now, Dr. Clark? In completing this prework, you are requested to provide a full and inclusive review, and a statement of actions that should be taken.

Teamwork. Teams are to develop criteria for a full and inclusive response to the case. These criteria will be shared in an open forum general session. At that session, the discussion will focus on four points: What are the critical features of this case? What principles of practice are illustrated in the incident? What actions should be taken? How could this problem have been avoided?

Critique. Individual prework will be exchanged between teams; coding will preserve the authors' identities. Teams will discuss each prework analysis and will write a brief critique for each author. [The brevity of this exercise precludes the authors' reading aloud their prework and critique to team colleagues.] The learning administrator will then distribute a model for a complete and full answer, previously prepared by the medical practitioners who wrote the case.

Summary

The implications of vocational and professional training for increased effectiveness are deep and far-reaching. As the examples in this chapter illustrate, synergogic designs permit a wide variety of performance effectiveness issues to be addressed in training. Unlike other educational methods, synergogy can be applied to the integrated learning of knowledge, attitudes, and skills. The three broad applications discussed in this chapter suggest directions toward which training can be developed.

9

〜〜〜〜〜〜〜〜

Applications
in Schools, Colleges,
and Universities

〜〜〜 To illustrate how synergogic designs can be applied
in formal educational settings, this chapter is devoted to extensive excerpts from a university course conducted by Dr. Charles
H. Hoke. Careful study of the instructions and instruments
should enable the reader to apply a similar format to a wide
variety of college and high school courses in which a standard
text is the basis for student learning.

Syllabus

The purpose of this course is to present the concepts and
practices of designing and evaluating information systems within a variety of organizations, following the general principles of
information resource management. Particular attention is given
to the systems development cycle of information systems and
how these systems should be managed and evaluated in an organizational setting.

Objectives

Students who successfully complete this course should
demonstrate a comprehensive understanding of the following
areas:

- a top-down view of information systems
- computer concepts, devices and information processing methods
- information systems concepts focusing on systems analysis, design, programming and implementation
- the systems development cycle, cost/benefit analysis, and management procedures
- management issues, such as styles of management, measuring effectiveness and productivity, and system selection

Method of Instruction

Classes are structured by a systems approach to adult education. This approach involves the student in team learning activities that focus on deepening understanding of information systems. In-class exercises provide a student-centered framework for thinking about and applying the concepts of information systems, including how they are developed, and managed.

Text

Chris Mader, *Information Systems: Technology, Economics, Application, Management* (Science Research Associates, Inc., 1979).
A bibliography will be provided in class.

Course Outline

Session 1: Introduction and overview
Session 2: Identifying information systems concepts
Session 3: Hardware and software
[Etc.]

TED for Identifying Information Systems Concepts

Schedule

Time	Activity
Prework	*Individual Preparation:* Reading chapters 1 and 2 of text; completion of multiple-choice test

Time	Activity
8:00–8:05	*General Session:* Orientation
8:05–9:25	*Team Activity:* Identifying information systems concepts
9:25–9:40	*General Session:* Scoring individual and team answers
9:40–9:55	*Team Activity:* Concept clarification
9:55–10:10	*Team Activity:* Teamwork critique
10:10–10:30	*Team Activity:* Generalizations
10:30–10:50	*Individual Activity:* Personal assessment

Objectives

The purposes of this activity are to: (1) identify the best answer to each of the thirty-three questions of the multiple-choice test on information systems concepts; (2) clarify areas of misunderstanding about information systems; (3) critique teamwork of this activity, and (4) evaluate comprehension of information systems.

Individual Preparation

Read chapters 1 and 2 of the text. Then, complete the multiple-choice test. The test questions will help you clarify your understanding of the ideas presented by the authors. You may refer to the text as you answer the questions. Your answers to these questions form the basis for discussion during the second session of this course. Therefore, it is important that you bring the completed test and the text to the second session of the course.

Select the one alternative that *best* completes the sentence, even though others may not be wrong. If you are unsure which answer is correct, it is better to leave the answer blank than to guess.

1. The importance of information to people is that
    A. with it they will make wiser decisions.
    B. it helps determine the financial condition of the organization.

    C.   it is essential to the functions of planning and control.

    D.   it is a source of power, authority, and control.

    E.   its quality and value determine the quality of decisions.

2.   The internal storage memory enables the computer to

    A.   process data.

    B.   simulate creative thought.

    C.   carry out a sequence of instructions.

    D.   recall mundane facts.

    E.   accomplish more than numeric calculations.

3.   The basis for evaluating information system performance is

    A.   the volume of data held in memory.

    B.   the rate of data throughout.

    C.   total costs.

    D.   the break-even point.

    E.   the degree to which the user's needs are met.

[Etc.]

Team Learning

Instructions. Each team is to identify the single best answer to each of the multiple-choice questions in the prework assignment. It may be helpful to have team members state their prework answers and reasons before coming to team agreement. It is also helpful if someone in the team records on a flip chart each person's answer. The text, *Information Systems,* is *not* to be consulted.

Individual prework and team answers are to be scored to measure and compare team results. The key for scoring is based on the content of the chapters in the text and will be distributed to you at the end of the team discussion. Correct answers are worth 3 points, incorrect answers minus 3 points, and unanswered items 0 points.

Although team members may change their minds as to which answer is correct, individual answers completed prior to this discussion should not be changed in prework as they will be used for scoring. Team answers should be recorded after one and one-half hours of discussion.

Scoring Key and Rationale for Correct Answers

1. A. Optimally, the final result of producing information is wise decision making, All other responses are correct but are less important than A.
2. E. The capacity for memory permits the computer to store data, either numeric or alpha symbols, that it can process in a variety of ways. Although all other answers are correct, E is the answer that best distinguishes a computer from simpler calculating machines.
3. E. The purpose of an information system is to enable the user to solve his or her problems. The degree of success in this endeavor is the measure of the system's value.

Scoring. The learning efficiency of each team will be determined.* With each team, there is the possibility of the team score exceeding any one of its members' scores, which indicates that team learning has produced understanding beyond that which even the best-prepared individual could have done alone.

Concept clarification. Read over the rationale for correct answers. As a team, discuss the questions you answered incorrectly. List any remaining areas of misunderstanding or disagreement for presentation at the next general session.

Teamwork critique. Using overall team performance and individual scores as indicators of learning effectiveness, team members can critique several aspects of learning. First, consider each individual's preparation. Did the individual study the multiple-choice test prior to reading the book? Did he or she answer selected questions while reading or was the test completed after the reading? Did he or she take notes, underline key points, and so on? Suggestions may be offered as to how each person might have increased the thoroughness of preparation.

*On computation of team learning efficiency, see Chapter Three, Figure 2.

A second focus of critique is to evaluate how team members worked together. Examples of behavior that can be discussed include:

- Was time managed so as to allow a sound and balanced discussion of all items?
- How even was the participation?
- How were conflicting points of view resolved?
- How did the team know when it had reached agreement (consensus, vote, chairman decision)?
- What can the team do to improve its effectiveness in the next team discussion?

Generalizations. Discuss the following questions and agree on a team answer:

1. What are the main reasons for using an information system? List several team conclusions.
2. What do you, as a team, imagine to be the biggest barrier to the successful implementation of information systems within organizations?
3. What are the four key measures of computer processing capability?
4. What is your attitude toward increased computerization?

Prepare a summary of the team's main points on a flip chart for presentation at the next general session. Select one person to act as a spokesperson for your team to present the team's conclusions in a report of five to ten minutes.

Personal Assessment

Each student, working alone, completes this test. Write *T* next to an item that is true, *F* if the item is false. The purpose is to evaluate your comprehension of the subject matter studied.

1. An example of a higher-level software is BASIC programming language.

2. In batch processing the key idea is the quality of the output is determined by the quality of input.
3. The index of computer costs per unit of performance has shown a steady decrease since 1945.
[Etc.]

TMTD for Hardware and Software

Schedule

Time	Activity
Prework	Individual preparation of designated text materials
8:00–8:05	*General Session:* Orientation
8:05–8:15	*Team Activity:* Prestudy prior to teamwork
8:15–9:15	*Team Activity:* Presentation of topics
9:15–9:25	*Team Activity:* Postpresentation study
9:25–9:45	*General Session:* Scoring
9:45–10:10	*Team Critique:* Individual feedback
10:10–10:30	*Team Critique:* Generalizations about hardware and software
10:30–10:50	*General Session:* Across-team comparisons

Objectives

The purposes of this activity are to: (1) study computer hardware and software by sharing responsibility for subject matter; (2) demonstrate each student's presentation style before participants; (3) gain feedback from others as to how each student's effectiveness in presenting subject matter could be increased; and (4) listen and help others in aiding them to present computer hardware and software subjects in a suitable manner.

Individual Preparation

As individual preparation, each team member is to study his or her part of the text, working alone. Team member A studies pages 49–65; member B, pages 65–75; member C, pages 76–94; D, pages 97–111; and E, pages 112–124.

As an individual team member, study your part and be prepared to present its contents to the other members of your team. During the presentation you will be explaining to the others your overall understanding and comprehension. You may use notes if you choose but not the text itself. When you are presenting your part, you should avoid adding content that is not in the text. However, if you do want to add something, let the others know when you depart from and return to the text.

Teamwork

Prestudy prior to teamwork. Prior to presenting material in teamwork, each person will meet with others assigned the same part—all A's from the teams convene as a study group, as do all B's, C's, and D's, and E's. Each study group should discuss how to best present the material so as to make the most effective use of the time available.

Presentation of topics. During this period, team members can work out procedures for ordering the presentations; the amount of time available to each presenter also may be agreed upon in advance. The arrangements can also specify whether members should reserve questions until after each presentation or if any member should be free to interrupt a presentation to ask for clarification. You may wish to build in checkpoints during which you will stop to consider the quality of progress, to introduce any needed changes to improve your procedure, and so on.

Postpresentation study. The prestudy teams of all the A's, all the B's, and so on will reconvene to review how well each person performed during team presentations. Each member can suggest how others might strengthen their preparation and communication skills.

Scoring. Each team's knowledge of all five parts will be evaluated in the following way. Each team member will individually complete a true-false test. Team members' average score will be the measure of your team's presentation and listening effectiveness.

Critique

Individual feedback. During this period teams will critique the presentations by individuals. First, each member will rate each presenter on eight characteristics:

• demonstrates thorough preparation
• listens attentively
• asks questions for clarification
• is open and direct in communicating
• pursues irrelevant details
• tends to dominate the floor
• gives few clues of understanding
• stays on the same wavelength

A three-point scale is used for these ratings:

1 = Excellent
2 = Satisfactory or Good
3 = Needs improvement

Ratings are then used to critique each member's contribution to the learning task and to offer suggestions for increasing effectiveness as a presenter and a listener.

After feedback is completed, write a brief answer to the following question: What did I learn about my presentation style and how might I increase my effectiveness?

Generalizations about hardware and software. Team members now discuss the following questions: (1) Does a manager need to know how computers work or just how to use them? (2) What are four important measures of performance for a data storage device? (3) By what measure of performance should input be evaluated?

Main points discussed are to be recorded on flip charts

for presentation at the next general session. Select one person to act as a spokesperson for your team to present the team's conclusions in a report of three to five minutes.

PJD for Systems Analysis

Schedule

Time	Activity
Prework (Session 1)	Individual preparation of a case study assignment
8:00–8:05	*General Session:* Introduction to performance judging
8:05–9:00	*Team Activity:* Developing team criteria
9:00–9:40	*General Session:* Criteria exchange and clarification
9:40–10:15	*Team Activity:* In-team comparison of criteria
10:15–10:50	*General Session:* Development of consolidated list of criteria
(Session 2)	
8:00–8:05	*General Session:* Orientation
8:05–9:20	*Team Activity:* Team discussion of schedule of changes
9:20–9:35	*Team Activity:* Summary of team critique
9:35–10:05	*Team Activity:* In-team comparison
10:05–10:25	*Team Critique:* Process critique
10:25–10:45	*Team Critique:* Generalizations regarding the systems analysis phase
10:45–10:50	*General Session:* Cross-team comparison

Objectives

The purposes of this activity are to: (1) develop skills in analyzing information system development problems; (2) study and perfect criteria for stating recommendations and justifications for changes to computerized information systems; (3) evaluate written recommendations prepared in advance against these criteria; (4) receive feedback from colleagues regarding

one's own performance in the context of the previously established criteria; and (5) offer each individual a critique of his or
her recommendations and improvement steps.

Individual Preparation

As preparation for the next session carefully review the
Old Jersey Bank case study. On the worksheet provided, write
your recommendations for a schedule of changes to the bank's
information systems; include your justifications for these recommendations. Give your completed answer sheet to the instructor at the beginning of the session.

Teamwork

Developing team criteria. Using the instructions in the
text for the systems analysis phase as a starting point, each team
is to discuss and agree among its members as to what constitutes an excellent schedule of changes for the Old Jersey Bank.
List the criteria on a flip chart.

Criteria exchange and clarification. Each team in turn will
present to the others its criteria for an excellent schedule of
changes. All criteria will then be discussed for purposes of clarification.

In-team comparison of criteria. Each team is to compare
its list of criteria with those of other teams, isolating areas of
agreement and disagreement. List areas of *disagreement* on a
flip chart for presentation at the next general session.

Development of consolidated list of criteria. Each team in
turn presents its areas of disagreement with the other teams.
These disagreements will then be examined, and teams will reason together to achieve a final set of criteria.

Judging Performance

Critique each of the individual worksheets assigned to
your team according to how excellent the statement is in terms

of the consolidated list of criteria. A suggested procedure for this critique follows.

Team discussion of schedule of changes. Each member takes administrative responsibility for one worksheet to be evaluated by the team. Member 1 takes worksheet A, member 2 takes worksheet B, and so on. Member 1 reads worksheet A aloud. Team members then critique the recommendations by comparing them to the consolidated list of criteria for an excellent schedule of changes. Member 1 takes notes on the team's consensus evaluation. Then proceed to the next worksheet.

Summary of team critique. After all worksheets have been discussed and evaluated, the member responsible for each worksheet summarizes the team critique in writing and returns the worksheet and written critique to the instructor. The worksheets are then returned to their authors.

In-team comparison. After the worksheets are returned, each member reads his or her own recommendations and the written critique to the team. Members may discuss the extent to which these written critiques offer insights on how to write an excellent schedule of changes to an information system.

As participants listen to the critiques, they should try to identify common themes. These themes are likely to be widely applicable and to represent basic generalizations that each member may productively take into consideration in writing systems analysis reports in the future.

Critique

Process critique. Team members can explore issues of defensiveness that arise in receiving feedback. Points of discussion might include: Were the written critiques accepted as valid? Did the quality of feedback differ when given anonymously (written critiques) and when given face to face (team discussion)?

Generalizations regarding the systems analysis phase. Prepare a brief summary (on newsprint) of your team's response to the following questions.

1. Usually 5 to 10 percent of the total work effort is devoted to defining systems objectives during the systems analysis phase. Why is this considerable investment of time so important?
2. Why is the systems analyst's job said to be the most crucial one in information systems? What mix of skills is required for effective performance?

CAD for Clarifying Attitudes About Computers

Schedule

Time	Activity
Prework	Individual completion of attitude items
8:00–8:05	*General Session:* Orientation
8:05–8:30	*Individual Activity:* Completion of attitude scale ranking
8:30–10:00	*Team Activity:* Ranking of "soundest"
10:00–10:10	*Team Activity:* Summarizing rankings
10:10–10:50	*General Session:* Report of team rankings and generalization

Objectives

The purposes of this activity are to: (1) determine the degree to which agreement exists within the adult community regarding the most desirable role for computers in our society; (2) clarify your attitudes as to fundamental issues in computers, software, and information systems; and (3) evaluate the extent to which community attitudes correspond with or are divergent from those held by individuals.

Individual Preparation

Write a brief description of your view of the ideal role of computers in relation to each of the following broad topics. Your answers should each be at least a sentence in length and describe your real feelings about the topic.

- the impact of computers on society
- computer myths
- control of information
- the value of information

Next, for the following four items, place a 5 by the choice that best represents an expression of your personal attitudes for what would be soundest. Number the other choices in order of descending preference.

1. The impact of computers on society:
    A. As time goes by computers will diminish in their general importance because of their dehumanizing effects on individuals, groups, and organizations.
    B. The computer will continue to affect and influence only those who use them in their jobs, such as engineers, scientists, and scholars.
    C. Eventually computer developments will produce robots and thinking machines that will replace most human labor and thus generate a race of people with an abundance of leisure time.
    D. The major adjustment will be that every citizen will have to change his lifestyle in some way as a consequence of the pervasive use of the computer.
    E. State and national governments will be primarily affected by computers because of the large cost of the equipment and programming; thus continual reorganizational efforts will result as greater organizational efficiency is sought.
    F. Only those who have the mental capability and education to understand the intricate circuitry, logic, and operation of the computer will be able to optimize its usage.
2. Computer myths:
    A. There is a general fear among people that the computer will displace people in some jobs, such as assembly-line work, clerical tasks, and telephone communications.

B. The many negative impressions people have concerning the computer can be neutralized through an understanding of the strengths and weaknesses of automated
systems.

C. Artificial intelligence programmed into the computer
will result in machines replacing humans in many decision-making roles.

D. Computer information systems of government and
business will eventually reduce or, at least, invade our
individual privacy and freedom.

E. Many people hold the view that errors in billing, in-
voicing, and checking accounts are caused by failures
in the computer system.

F. Because the computer can accomplish tasks more rap-
idly and accurately than humans, we can expect increasing unemployment.

3. Control of information:

A. Because of the complexity of computers and the designs for their use, only those professional experts
trained in computer science should control information systems.

B. Top- and middle-management levels should have primary responsibility for planning, implementing, and
controlling information processing functions.

C. A data processing group responsible for information
processing should be under a senior official, such as a
financial vice-president.

D. Data processing professionals should be distributed
throughout an organization in all departments and
units that utilize information systems.

E. The design, operation, and control of information processing is a management concern of the total organization.

F. In view of the need for information security, protect-
ing organizational strategies and policies, and maintaining a favorable competitive posture, information
must be controlled at a central place in the organization.

4. The value of information:
   A. In reality, information is cheap, perishable, and has only a relatively low worth as compared to people and material.
   B. Since only people generate and use information, the value of information resides in its usefulness to individuals rather than its organizational value.
   C. Computerized information must be considered as a valuable organizational resource.
   D. Information stored in computers is of primary value to computer specialists and immediate users of these systems.
   E. Information is often used in a subtle way by people to protect their position, expertise, or power.
   F. Information is of principal value to top management who have the motivation and responsibility for achievement of organization goals.

Teamwork

Ranking of soundest. As a team, reach agreement on an ideal ranking for questionnaire items 1 through 4. *Soundest* here means that the ranking of alternatives is from *6*, the attitude that would be most conducive to more efficient and effective use of computers, to *1*, the attitude that would be least conducive.

Each team member could in turn explain the ranking selected for item 1 and the rationale for this ranking. As the reasons for each item ranking are discussed, personal attitudes toward particular issues form the basis for arriving at soundest attitudes. A record of individual and team rankings should be kept for summary and generalization purposes.

Summarizing rankings. Each team is asked to report its agreed-on rankings. These will be summarized on a blackboard or on a flip chart to illustrate similarities and differences between team rankings. Teams will then examine the reasoning that yielded the rankings.

10

❦ ᴄ◌ᴄ◌ᴄ◌ᴄ◌ᴄ◌◌ ᴄᴏ

Synergogy

Future Directions for Education, Training, and Development

❦ᴄ◌◌ Educators and trainers encounter many different attitudes toward learning among their students and trainees. It is something of a rarity to find a group of learners who are keenly involved, actively participating, and deeply committed to their own learning. Some educators have dismissed that kind of participation as a realistic objective. Others remain convinced that learning can and should be exciting and rewarding, and they believe that these motivations are essential for real learning to occur.

Learner-centered education holds the promise of increasing learners' involvement, participation, and commitment—but it must be directed in such a way that standards of excellence are maintained and learning outcomes are assured. As we have discussed throughout this book, synergogy provides a structure for learner-centered education that enables learners to exercise responsibility and initiative in a setting that both supports and guides their autonomy.

In this chapter we present edited transcripts of interviews with educators who have used synergogic designs. These interviews focus on the three basic elements of synergogic methods—learning designs and instruments, teamwork, and synergy in learning—responses of the educators and their students,

160

and learning outcomes. An interview with the senior trainer in a large industrial organization is presented first, followed by interviews with two university professors and an elementary school teacher.

Industrial Training

Q: How long have you been using synergogy?

A: About six or seven years.

Q: Which of the basic four designs seems the most popular and effective?

A: At present, I would say there is very little difference among them in terms of application. The TED finds more universal favor. Initially, it was the CAD that people latched on to, with the PJD the last to take off. I think it's worth noting that a number of combinations of the basic designs are in use, such as a CAD followed by a TED for a specific purpose, or a TED with a PJD when we establish criteria for effective objective writing after dealing with the conceptual issues in approaching training from an outcomes orientation.

Q: Why the initial interest in CAD?

A: We were concerned about attitude formation and attitude change as our company was shifting its tempo. We used it for things like equal opportunity, legislation regarding health and safety at work, and so on.

Q: Any negative responses to the CAD?

A: When I did my first presentation on this to the advisory committee, which includes the union with its educational and other interests, they feared that the CAD was possibly some sort of Machiavellian brainwashing operation, that the company was trying to indoctrinate employees, so to speak. Yet I know of no instances of designs being used in that way, and it's no longer a problem or worry.

Q: Do you see the CAD as a means for trainees to self-check attitudes at the beginning and then at the end of the learning experience?

A: It is certainly used in that way, very often in conjunction with some knowledge or skill design.

Q: What do you see as the main strengths and advantages of the TED?

A: If the material is such that, after studying it, people are likely to take opposing views about various issues, that lends itself to the TED more than material that is clear-cut and absolutely definite. As another example, the marketing area is a useful subject for a TED learning design. Whereas material on legislation or a fixed procedure is often so turgid and boring that we use the TMTD to reduce the amount of solo study and to enliven the learning situation through discussion. The TMTD is also useful when the material is readily divisible into the appropriate number of chunks. When items to be tested are either factually correct, in accordance with the rules or procedures, or incorrect—that's when the TMTD is probably better than TED.

Q: Is the time factor in administering a design significant—the fact that it may take longer than a lecture?

A: It could be, but many people using the TED will tell you that if you possibly can have the trainee students complete the prework before going to a course, then you save a bit of time. You've also got to bear in mind that you are not merely dispensing knowledge, but you are to a degree testing trainees' understanding of it as well. I think the users of TEDs across the industry have found that the quality of learning is such that if the training objectives require higher-quality understanding then any extra time taken by the TED in comparison to lectures seems worthwhile.

Q: For a successful TED, don't you need a soundly written document?

A: Absolutely. I'd say that a sound document and a very sound multiple-choice test are basic. Writing the multiple-choice test is hard, very skilled work. It is more difficult to write multiple-choice items for the TED than for a straight-forward attainment test. The distractors have to be such that genuine discussion can be generated, whereas in a simple validation test, as long as you have one distractor that's a pretty near miss, and as long as the remaining distractors aren't too wild, you would still validly test that learning point. We need something rather more sophisticated in the TED.

Q: Is comparison scoring, which generates competition between teams, useful?

A: It depends on the subject you are dealing with. Scoring is a constructive activity when you want to generate good teamwork. On the other hand, if a TED is a knowledge-acquisition part of a training exercise and what follows is practical work that is not going to be done in teams, then I am more doubtful about the added value of comparison scoring.

Q: What about TMTD?

A: TMTD is widely used with people who need more than an appreciation of legislation and procedures, that is, people who need a working knowledge of a subject so that they can make judgments and say, "This is the right way, and that is the wrong way." We use it for safety, consumer protection legislation, employment protection, and personnel practices. As far as procedures are concerned, TMTD is very useful when fairly important rules have to be learned, such as in marketing, stock control, stores, or customer billing.

An interesting point here is that rather difficult-to-follow procedures manuals have to be virtually rewritten in order to make the message clear. This has made us all aware of the importance of clear writing and how often our manuals are not all that clear. This is a brilliant discipline, in my judgment. We put the rewritten material in front of the specialists, such as lawyers or accountants, to get their reactions. They often then become aware of the obscurities characteristic of their own writings. Not always, though, because a few will say, "Oh, you've oversimplified." But there are usually no problems as long as one makes it clear to the specialist that the rewritten material concerns, say, consumer protection law as it affects the performance of a customer service representative not as it affects a lawyer who is likely to be pleading a case in court. After revising the technical materials to make them fully understandable, we may go back to the "legal eagles" to review the true-false test for accuracy.

Another use of TMTD is in areas where there are very often quite severe penalties for errors in application.

Q: Do you find true-false items difficult to write?

A: They are easier than multiple-choice items, but they are still difficult. One crucially important aspect of the design work is identifying the major learning points. What is really important? What is trivial? A well-prepared base manuscript doesn't really have any trivial points, but this only became clear to us as a result of the instruments needed to administer the designs. There is, however, the danger of redundancy testing, that is, testing the same learning point twice. You have to guard against that.

Q: What about the disadvantage of expecting people to teach each other?

A: I think for those who have the skill and confidence to use it, and with a good instrument, good source material, good true-false items, and so on, the TMTD is the most powerful motivator you can have for preparation. When individuals realize that they are responsible for their teammates' learning, it concentrates them unmercifully. People genuinely want to help their colleagues if they can. Also, they enjoy it.

Q: Have you had to review material because people have not learned well from a TMTD or has a certain section been particularly difficult so that people have done rather badly on the true-false questions?

A: I haven't noticed that sort of problem.

Q: What has been your experience with the PJD?

A: It was the least used to start with, but it's used more now. Initially, it was for skills like letter writing and report writing, or interviewing, subjects that would naturally lend themselves to it.

The breakthrough came about three years ago when

criteria for design became the subject matter for a variety of settings—commercial gas installations, restaurant kitchens, central heating in offices, and so on. There are now about four or five PJDs on design subjects where the criteria for effective design have to be established. From given data, trainees actually do a design and subsequently determine the criteria for sound design and then compare their own efforts against the design criteria. The learning of the criteria is what strengthens the final product, not simply practice in going directly to design work. It's really good in those areas.

Q: Was the PJD used least initially because it was seen as most difficult?

A: Yes, I think so. The historical attitudes of the teacher-tell orientation made trainers reluctant to accept that trainees, particularly young people, would, in fact, be able to establish criteria. But through trying they realized that such lack of experience is much more likely to encourage people to adopt criteria for effectiveness—in whatever skill it happens to be—that are much more rigorous than you would ever dare impose. The sort of designs I'm talking about are things like workshop practices for apprentices. Initial doubts about the ability of very young people to develop criteria have proved unfounded.

Q: How can you be sure that the criteria meet a predetermined standard?

A: The only point at which a subject-matter expert check is needed is when the criteria are finally determined. If a fundamentally important thing is omitted, participants have to see the option and accept it as one of their criteria.

Q: Is there any student resistance to PJD?

A: It would be wrong to call it resistance. There is some surprise; someone will say, "Why didn't you tell us the criteria when you knew them all along," and that sort of thing. Another reaction is, "Why go to all this trouble when in the past we've just been lectured on this." But on the whole, responses are positive, certainly in terms of enjoyment.

Q: Any general comments on synergogy that you think worth passing on?

A: I think of synergogy as a range of student-centered, training-centered strategies with enormous potential. Go into almost any training center anywhere and into any workshop in our company, and even if a basic design isn't being conducted you will find some sort of synergogic influence —better texts, better tests, more participation, that sort of thing.

Q: I think you also said it probably has made people think more creatively about the way they are teaching.

A: Yes, about the really important things. First of all, what population are you dealing with? What skills, knowledge, attitudes do they need to have that they don't have at the moment? What ought to be the strategies for helping them acquire what they need? How are we going to test whether the goals that we've set have been achieved? All those things are part of synergogic designs, and they have influenced the teaching of subjects for which we haven't used synergogic models.

Graduate School Courses

Q: How long have you used synergogic designs in teaching graduate students?

A: I have taught for many years but I began experimenting with the synergogy designs about six years ago. Now all my courses are carried out that way.

Q: What's your overall reaction?

A: I love it, personally. I find it very satisfying as a way of conducting classroom learning, particularly the growth in personal effectiveness I observe in students as they blossom. My other reaction is that synergogy renders much of the academic approach somewhat antiquated because it makes "teachers out of students" and designers out of teachers, and that's not exactly what drew many of us into teaching in the first place, and it's not what many students conceive of as being a student.

Q: In terms of student endorsement, can you rank the designs for popularity with students?

A: I think the TED comes first. I give a TED at the beginning and repeatedly over the first several weeks of the semester, a twenty-item multiple-choice test. Results are usually very poor. By midterm, do they turn on! In my last class teams went way off the scale—70 percent learning efficiency in one team, 75 percent in another, and I had two perfect scores, which I never get. They loved it. A woman turned around to me a couple of times and said, "This is really great. This really does it."

I've been using TMTD at lot, but mainly because I want them to get through some indispensable material that is rather boring, and available only in pretty tough books. With TMTD, the text becomes important, almost as a means toward the end—helping each other get to know what they need to know in a sound way without everyone having to read the same material. It's second in popularity, because of the process but it also compels them to grasp a lot of dull but essential material that would be difficult for everyone to plug through alone. The fun of the design compensates for the dullness of the material. TED is more popular because it places more reliance on thinking and judgment and less on book detail.

Q: What about the PJD?

A: The PJD is powerful and I use it either with case studies or report writing. I have them take the case study home, write out their response, and bring it to class. When they do teamwork the first time around, they have difficulty in developing criteria. They can't believe that *they're* supposed to develop the criteria. They keep looking at me as if saying, "Well, gosh, aren't you the expert? Aren't you the one that decides all this?" Each time I have to discuss their expectations of being "told" before they can feel comfortable in working within the design framework; but once they begin to think in terms of criteria for judging effectiveness, it turns out to be a very intellectually maturing source of insight.

Q: Have you used the CAD very much?

A: I've used it in the beginning of the course and on a pre-post basis too. It's stimulating and it gives them something to really get their teeth into. I like it too. Yet it's hard writing those scales.

Q: Do students complain about the way the courses are being conducted?

A: Not as a rule. They seem to accept it as natural and most enjoy it as a fun way of learning. But that's not always so. The ones who complain are the "children" who expect to be spoon-fed; they want to be told what to do. It's quite surprising to see students who are threatened by the need to participate.

Q: Can you give me an example of a complaint?

A: One woman objected the first thing out of the hatch. She called me on the phone and asked, "What's this all about? This looks like a bunch of baloney. I'm supposed to do this and this. When are you going to teach us something?" I talked to her a long time and in a somewhat confronting way. I said, "Look, Mary, I want you to develop and I want you to act like a graduate student who is competent to deal with others face-to-face. I want you to develop some intense thinking, to learn to be more critical, and to become more comfortable in thinking on your feet and expressing yourself to others so they'll understand what you are trying to convey. You, all of us, need to be able to think critically and express ourselves clearly whether we go into industry, government, or teaching. That is what this class is all about." Once I gave her a rationale for what she might gain from taking more responsibility for herself and others, she was just great, and she's been great ever since. She's first in the program now. When students see what's involved, they take to it. I think university students *expect* to be *taught,* more than industrial students who may be more motivated to learn.

Q: Do they come around eventually?

A: Oh, yes, they do come around, but I had one student who did not come around very quickly. Some who show improvement change from being very low in comprehension and confidence at the beginning to being at the top by the end—it is a glorious experience.

Q: Let me ask about your role as a learning administrator. You said that your keeping out of the discussion creates a problem for some students because they keep looking to you for help to teach them. What is the most common issue in which you deliberately intervene rather than being called upon?

A: I have to intervene to deal with individual behavior problems. For example, Tom was mad at me in the beginning because he said I wasn't teaching him anything. Finally, I had to lead him into the hall and really put it to him. He hadn't done any study and he wanted to sit in the class and take notes. I said, "Look, Tom, this is a different approach. You've got to do the prestudy, and you've got to be responsible for helping your teammates learn something." He was just great for the rest of the course.

Q: Any others?

A: The last time I intervened was just this last week. I was out of the room doing something else and left three study teams—eighteen people—working. The room had no barriers or partitions between teams. It was a tough exercise to complete and when I walked back in two male students were in a shouting match. I didn't have to do much because there's no question that students recognize me as an authority figure whether they like it or not, or whether I like it or not. I just said, "Look, let's knock this off. This is ridiculous. You ruin it for the rest of the people in the class." That's all I had to say.

Q: What kind of secondary gains do you see—increased skills in teamwork? improved personal self-confidence?

A: Both, but let me be specific. I've got another student who is employed full-time but doing independent study with me. I see her on Saturdays in the morning. Pat was in my class a couple of years ago. She was very shy and very quiet, kind of nervous. She'd come up to me after a TED and say, "Gee, I hate these tests. They make me nervous."

I talked with her about her tenseness. She saw her problem as not being able to communicate as well as she would like. I saw it as shyness—she speaks quite well once she gets over her sense of embarrassment. I told her that her job as an adult learner was to learn how to communicate more spontaneously. After a few little talks with her and after her experiments—which the designs stimulated—in being more effective, she became more confident. Now she's doing advanced graduate work and doing very well as a data process manager. She's told me that the personal effectiveness she learned from completing the designs helped her get such a good job; that the job was a direct result of the teamwork designs in that course.

Q: What kinds of demands does writing designs make compared to lecturing?

A: I love writing designs, but I don't mind lecturing either. I'm so absorbed in using the synergogy designs that I lighten up on lecturing. I just have a certain amount of time, two and a half hours, per session, and every bit of that is filled with one of the parts of each design. The only lecturing I do is impromptu.

Q: Would you go back to using a straight lecture method for the courses you are teaching now?

A: Only if the synergogy option were unavailable. I'm so rewarded by the growth of student interest in the subject matter as well as in their personal and interpersonal effectiveness that I can't lecture in good conscience. Probably I would if somebody said that's the only thing I could do for the rest of my life, but I'm not going to do it on my own initiative. When they ask me to teach a new course, I just sit down and start outlining the design. The better the design, the less the students realize the effort that has gone into it. From their point of view, it all looks so easy.

Q: What's the most difficult part of the design work?

A: Writing a TED multiple-choice test. It's hard to get those choices. I can get the stem, and getting the right answer is no problem. But getting that second, third, fourth, and fifth statement at the right level of discrimination is the hard step. The true-false tests don't bother me at all.

Q: Student reactions are one thing, and certainly any contribution of education to enhancing interpersonal competence is another, but the justification for education is related to the acquisition of knowledge, learning to think, and the like. Can you evaluate synergogy compared with more traditional classroom approaches?

A: I've done controlled experiments and as far as objective data are concerned, students learning by synergogic designs come out as well or better than those who learn the same subject matter through lecture and discussion. If you consider the "whole learner" concept, I find that synergogy results in a more rapid maturing of intellectual capacity.

Q: What about the reactions of other faculty members?

A: I've had some difficulty with other faculty. Some see me working with students in a nontraditional manner and they interpret it as "shortchanging" the students. But when I invite them to review the whole approach, that often resolves their concerns. How would you handle it?

Q: The entire department learns the process in a synergogy seminar first, and then one or two people are asked to start a small experiment or two. Then everyone understands the process, can interpret its effect and even recommend the next steps. It's the only way I can think of to *reduce* resistance to change at the beginning.

A: That certainly would be better than to try to *overcome* resistance later on.

Q: What's your overall evaluation?

A: I'm thrilled with the possibilities. One design opens up the opportunity to help students examine their attitudes, another to explore the ultimate importance of learning criteria for the evaluation of action; a third aids them to acquire presentation skills, and the fourth to think more subtly and to make more precise discriminations. All those are important. But beyond that, TED and TMTD help students to study, to think about what they are studying, to explain it to others, and to engage in give-and-take on a variety of subjects. Conventional education has not been very successful in helping students acquire the skills to critique and to share with their classmates in ways that help them become more personally effective.

For me the greatest reward is in seeing students who enter the classroom with a passive orientation, often taking a course only because it is required for a degree or a vocation, become involved in learning the subject matter and involved with one another. These designs open up a new set of meanings for the words *participation* and *education,* and synergogy provides a total system for students to strengthen their personal and interpersonal competence.

Undergraduate Courses

Q: Have you used these approaches with college students?

A: Yes. I've used the designs with different undergraduate students and they've worked phenomenally well. Students learned at least three times as much as they would have if I had just lectured and so forth. All kinds of reinforcers come into play. Of course, part of the reason that they learn more is that they study more and prepare better.

Q: For example?

A: I might take six chapters that they are supposed to know perfectly. Then, I prepare twelve discussion or essay questions, a pair for each chapter. One of each pair is for the study team and the other is used as an exam that individuals work on alone. I have a procedure for them selecting their own team composition, and then building norms, and studying their group process. The teams decide who is to teach each of the chapters and answer the question that corresponds to the chapter. Then I do a re-teaming where all the people working on a designated portion get together and pool their knowledge. In this way they work out a good answer for their assigned question and are prepared to teach their chapter to the members of their original team. At the end, everyone completes the alternative set of essay questions to evaluate learning.

I have pretty elaborate kinds of reinforcers for helping them achieve their best. I encourage members to think of how to get everyone involved. They call each other at night, talk to people who are absent from class, and so on. It produces quite a different learning climate than is possible with pedagogy.

Q: What problems have you encountered?

A: Some of the teams bomb. Some people will sabotage anything. Then I have to intervene with individuals or maybe even recompose teams.

Q: Does student-centered learning deprive you of the gratification that can come from being the center of the class' attention?

A: Yes, I've experienced that. I would be dying to give some lecture that they could say "oh and ah," or "Oh, yes, I think you're right." But I've learned to control that need on my part.

Q: Are you ever tempted to intervene when students reach a temporary impasse rather than letting them clear it up?

A: It has to do with how you diagnose the team's actual difficulty and members' potential for solving it. These are individual differences, of course, but I don't think it's too much of a problem.

Q: How do other faculty respond to what you are doing with synergogy?

A: Some of them love it. It is a very popular approach, though I think there is some resentment, too. If my entire class received A's or B's, there was quite a bit of comment from some faculty members that I was just giving high grades so the students would like me. But when I have shown the essay tests to other professors, they say the answers are phenomenal. In one case, we all gave the same essay final, coded the papers and distributed them for grading to professors using different models for teaching. When we decoded them, all of us agreed that the students who had learned in the synergogic designs had excelled in comparison with the others.

Q: Complaints from students?

A: Oh, the usual. Some complain that they do too much work, and that I don't lecture to them and really teach them things. There are those kinds of complaints, but they are minor.

Elementary School Classes

Q: To what degree do the designs promote enthusiasm or resistance in your elementary school students?

A: The fifth-graders are just quite enthusiastic, particularly about TMTD. We also have used it with some sixth-graders. We train a lot of teachers who are both fifth- and sixth-grade teachers. We even use it in some lower classes and in quite a few junior high and high school classes, too. Of course the teachers who use it are fairly good teachers but the kids enjoy it. There's a lot of social rewards.

Q: What about teasing, squabbling, and arguing?

A: Those problems decrease as the ages of participants increase; more intervention to maintain a sense of order is needed for fifth-grade than for tenth-grade students. As group members become more experienced, they are increasingly able to keep their own members in line.

Q: Is the TMTD conducted in a leaderless way?

A: Not necessarily. Aronson and others (1978) recommend the designation and training of group leaders for teams of fifth- and sixth-graders; these students serve almost as teacher surrogates, particularly until team members have learned to manage themselves. Then the group leader may be rotated or one may not be needed. With even younger children, Johnson and Johnson (1975) use a procedure that assigns each child a certain role to guide his or her participation.

Q: Can you compare the rate of learning and knowledge acquisition between the traditional classroom model and the TMTD?

A: My guess is that the results probably have as much to do with the teacher as with the method. With a good teacher, I think that the students learn more with the TMTD's cooperative approach.

Q: Do you notice that teachers intervene a lot in the elementary school groups?

A: Yes. The fifth-grade teachers intervene fairly strongly. They really help control it [provide guidance when students need help in discussion because they lack process skills], particularly early on. With elementary teachers, it's a little hard to say whether they intervene more or less than in the regular classroom. Teachers are really important in the way they move around and work with the groups. The real issue is to help teachers become effective in implementing synergogic designs, which can provide a framework for maintaining order in the classroom without the excessive exercise of direct authority.

The teachers say the atmosphere in the classroom is very important. They help by doing things that build trust, of which TMTD is one. We have structured questions for use in the synergogic designs that provide internal controls. Students spend five or so minutes talking with each other about who did what well, how they can improve working together, and so on. Teachers ought to pay more attention to the group process because it makes a big difference in the feelings the kids develop for one another.

To this interview, let us append several observations about applications of synergogy in public school classes. A recent federal report on education, *A Nation at Risk* (Gardner, 1983), concludes that public education can be improved if traditional pedagogy is improved. But experience with synergogic designs in the public schools suggests that synergogy may prove to be a constructive alternative to reformed pedagogy.

Variations of the TED and the TMTD are the designs most often used, with the TMTD the more frequently employed. A variety of subjects have been taught using synergogic methods, including social studies, mathematics, and language arts. Teams usually have five or six students, most often grouped heterogeneously with respect both to task ability on the subject and to race or ethnicity. The standard arrangement for using synergogic designs is two hours a day for a six-week period.

Some applications have been subjected to experimental analyses significantly beyond the acquisition of the subject matter itself. These experimental designs have compared students of equivalent abilities taught by either synergogic designs or the standard classroom model. Aronson and others (1978) report three conclusions: (1) The best students learn equally well under either condition; poorer students learn significantly more from the synergogic designs than from the standard classroom model. (2) Self-esteem is enhanced among all levels of students using synergogic designs. (3) Comparisons of the number of cross-racial friendships made by students before and after their classes show that a significantly larger number of such friendships are made by students in synergogic classroom settings than in standard classrooms. (For further discussion, see DeVries, Edwards, and Slavin, 1978; Johnson and Johnson, 1975.)

Implications

The importance of synergogy for the future of education can be briefly summarized. First and foremost is the prospect that synergogy can accelerate the rate at which true learning occurs—an objective sufficient to justify placing increased reliance on this approach to education.

Over and above the cognitive or substantive learning outcomes, however, are the contributions that team-based learning offers individuals in acquiring the social interaction skills so important to their personal effectiveness. Certainly, one of the goals of education is to help individuals work effectively together in finding best solutions to problems they face, whether at work or at home.

Again, quite apart from the subject matter studied during synergogic learning experiences, synergogic learning has implications for managerial competence and organization effectiveness. As individuals learn the *processes* of teamwork, stronger and more effective participation is possible, which in turn improves management. Individuals learn that they can work together, keep themselves on track, resolve their differences, and reach conclusions without anyone being formally designated the leader who exercises control over the rest. A related insight that participants gain is that the *quality* of contributions that individuals have to offer is not particularly related to their rank. Both of these realizations work together to produce improved problem solving and decision making on the job.

Another implication of synergogy is related to the administrative and professional arrangements for education. In traditional pedagogy, the teacher is central, and much of the educational apparatus is calculated to serve the teacher-student relationship in the classroom. But, as we have seen, the problems inherent in pedagogy will not be remedied by strengthening the traditional teacher-student relationship through smaller classes, better pay for teachers, or more audiovisual or even computerized equipment. Such activities can be expected to do little more than edge us toward bankruptcy at an accelerated rate and on a national scale.

In contrast, synergogy introduces a basic reorientation in regard to the concepts of *teacher* and *classroom*. The need for experts is not abolished, but fewer are needed because each expert's contribution is made through learning instruments and designs that can be widely implemented by less-specialized learning administrators, who also provide the orientation and supervision. There are important financial implications here in that teacher-student ratio is no longer a relevant concern, since the immediate learning environment is a team of four to eight persons. Yet, as we have seen, synergogy retains the unique advantages of pedagogy and andragogy, while avoiding their weaknesses.

Significant evidence points to two fundamental shifts in American culture as the year 2000 approaches. We are returning to fundamental concepts of competence, and we are moving toward excellence through effective participation. Synergogy permits fundamentals to be the object of learning through means that stimulate the learner's involvement and commitment in strengthening their competencies. Beyond the acquisition of knowledge, synergogy provides a means for studying and rectifying many real-life problems related to attitudes as well as for acquiring skills requisite to the effective application of competencies in all aspects of an individual's life.

Selected Annotated Bibliography

∞〰〰〰〰〰∞

In addition to the following works, the reader may wish to consult the extensive social psychology literature on small-group action learning. Although most of this literature does not include structured programs to motivate and guide learners, the reader will find suggestions that can be adapted to vary the four basic synergogic designs.

Aronson, E. and others. *The Jigsaw Classroom*. Beverly Hills, Calif.: Sage, 1978.

The authors report on the Team-Member Teaching Design in applications at the elementary school level. The design is referred to as a "jigsaw group" because each student has a piece of the total puzzle to contribute to the group's overall understanding. In addition to discussing the use of the design in the elementary setting, the authors present research conclusions comparing the design with a standard classroom model based on traditional pedagogy. These conclusions concern the effects of synergogy on knowledge acquisition as well as social consequences that the design produces. Among the significant changes

179

reported are students' increased self-esteem and increased inter-racial friendship choices following synergogy in comparison with the standard classroom model.

DeVries, D. L., Edwards, K. J., and Slavin, R. E. "Bi-Racial Learning Teams and Race Relations in the Classroom: Four Field Experiments on Teams-Games-Tournament." *Journal of Educational Psychology,* 1978, 7,(3), 356–362.

The authors conducted a series of studies in elementary classrooms that combined within-group cooperation with across-group competition. Their conclusions are comparable to those reached by Aronson and others (1978).

Johnson, D. W., and Johnson, R. T. *Learning Together and Alone.* Englewood Cliffs, N.J.: Prentice-Hall, 1975.

Johnson and Johnson report the results of experiments using classroom group settings similar in several respects to both the Team Effectiveness Design and the Team-Member Teaching Design. Their conclusions address the effect of the learning method on knowledge acquisition and other sociological variables.

Knowles, M. *The Adult Learner: A Neglected Species.* Houston: Gulf Publishing Company, 1973.

Knowles defines the andragogic model of adult learning and compares it with pedagogical approaches. This book also introduces the interested reader to extensive psychological research on the conditions conducive to learning, without particular reference to the strategy of instruction.

Blake, Robert, R., and Mouton, Jane S. "The Instrumented Training Laboratory." In I. R. Weschler and E. H. Schein (Eds.), *Issues in Training.* Selected Reading Series 5.

Washington, D.C.: National Training Laboratories, 1962, pp. 61–76.

This article is of historical interest since it first introduced the idea of synergogy.

Revans, R. W. *The Origins and Growth of Action Learning.* Lund, Sweden: Studentlitteratur, 1982.

Revans reports on the research and practice he conducted over many years on a method called "action learning." Action learning takes place in small groups under conditions that enable participants to examine and reinterpret the agreements and disagreements that emerge among participants as they discuss the subject matter under study. Revans draws implications for the induction of institutional change as well as evaluating this approach for the acquisition of subject matter.

References

Alcoholics Anonymous (Rev. ed.) New York: AA Publishing, 1955.

Aronson, E., and others. *The Jigsaw Classroom.* Beverly Hills, Calif.: Sage, 1978.

Blake, R. R., and Mouton, J. S. "The Instrumented Training Laboratory." In I. R. Weschler and E. H. Schein (Eds.), *Issues in Training.* Selected Reading Series 5. Washington, D.C.: National Training Laboratories, 1962, pp. 61–76.

Blake, R. R., and Mouton, J. S. *How to Maximize the Integration of Organization Components.* San Francisco: Jossey-Bass, forthcoming.

DeVries, D. L., Edwards, K. J., and Slavin, R. E. "Bi-Racial Learning Teams and Race Relations in the Classroom: Four Field Experiments on Teams-Games-Tournament." *Journal of Educational Psychology,* 1978, 7(3), 356–362.

Enright, J. B. "On the Playing Fields of Synanon." In L. Blank, G. B. Gottsegen, and M. G. Gottsegen (Eds.), *Confrontation: Encounters in Self and Interpersonal Awareness.* New York: Macmillan, 1971.

Gardner, D. T. *A Nation at Risk.* Report of the National Committee on Excellence in Education. Washington, D.C.: U.S. Government Printing Office, 1983.

Gartner, A., Kohler, M., and Riessman, F. *Children Teach Children.* New York: Harper & Row, 1971.

Hallowitz, E. "The Expanding Role of the Neighborhood Service Center." In F. Riessman and H. R. Popper (Eds.), *Up From Poverty: New Career Ladders for Nonprofessionals.* New York: Harper & Row, 1968.

Johnson, D. W., and Johnson, R. T. *Learning Together and Alone.* Englewood Cliffs, N.J.: Prentice-Hall, 1975.

Knowles, M. *The Adult Learner: A Neglected Species.* Houston: Gulf Publishing Company, 1973.

Laubach, F. C., and Laubach, R. I. *Toward World History.* Syracuse, N.Y.: Syracuse University Press, 1960.

Low, A. A. *Mental Health Through Will-Training: A System of Self-Help in Psychotherapy as Practiced by Recovery, Incorporated.* (14th ed.) Boston: Christopher Publishing House, 1966.

Mead, M. *Coming of Age in Samoa.* New York: New American Library, 1949.

Mouton, J. S., and Blake, R. R. "University Training in Human Relations Skills." In L. P. Bradford (Ed.), *Human Forces in Teaching and Learning.* Washington, D.C.: National Training Laboratories, National Education Association, 1961.

Neill, A. S. *Summerhill: A Radical Approach to Child Rearing.* New York: Hart, 1960.

Nyquist, E. B., and Hawes, G. R. *Open Education.* New York: Bantam Books, 1972.

Revans, R. W. *The Origins and Growth of Action Learning.* Lund, Sweden: Studentlitteratur, 1982.

Riessman, F. "The Helper Therapy Principle." *Social Work,* 1965, *10*(2), 27-32.

Index

❧⸱✦⸱✦⸱✦⸱☙